THEY WROTE ABO[UT]
A collection of biogra[phies]

With illustrations by the author

by
RICHARD KNOWLES

COUNTRY BOOKS

First published in 2003 by Country Books,
Courtyard Cottage, Little Longstone, Bakewell,
Derbyshire DE45 INN, England

ISBN I 898941 81 5

© 2003 Richard Knowles (text & illustrations)

The rights of Richard Knowles as author of this work has
been asserted by him in accordance with the
Copyright, Designs & Patents Act 1993

All rights reserved. No part of this publication may be reproduced,
stored in a retrieval system or transmitted in any form or by any
means, electronic, mechanical, photocopying, recording or otherwise,
without the prior permission of the publisher and copyright holder.

Printed and bound by:
Antony Rowe Ltd, Eastbourne

Contents

Introduction		5
Arthur Beckett	(1871-1943)	6
Hilaire Belloc	(1870-1953)	11
N.P. Blaker	(1835-1920)	15
E. Cecil Curwen	(1895-1967)	20
Howard Dudley	(1820-1864)	23
Tickner Edwardes	(1865-1944)	26
J. Coker Egerton	(1829-1888)	30
Edward Boys Ellman	(1815-1906)	34
A.A. Evans	(1862-1946)	39
Thomas Geering	(1813-1889)	43
T.W. Horsfield	(1792-1837)	45
W.H. Hudson	(1841-1922)	49
Richard Jefferies	(1848-1887)	54
Mark Anthony Lower	(1813-1876)	58
Richard Lower	(1782-1865)	61
E.V. Lucas	(1868-1938)	64
Gideon Algernon Mantell	(1790-1852)	68
Esther Hallam Meynell	(1890-1955)	75
W.D. Parish	(1863-1904)	80
Maude Robinson	(1859-1950)	84
George Forrester Scott [John Halsham]	(1853-1937)	87
Sir Charles Thomas-Stanford	(1858-1932)	90
Thomas Turner	(1729-1793)	94
Barclay Wills	(1877-1962)	99
Frances, Viscountess Wolseley	(1872-1936)	104
Gerard Young	(1912-1972)	109
Bibliography		113
Sources		115
Envoi		120
Index of Sussex place-names		122

INTRODUCTION

"No County in England has been more written about than Sussex." That was the opinion of Arthur Beckett when he launched *The Sussex County Magazine* in December 1926. A decade later George Aitchison wrote: "Of the making of Sussex books there in no end." There is still no end to the making of Sussex books, more of them appear every year, and some like *The South Downs* by Peter Brandon, which was published in 1998, seem sure to take their place among the county's classics. Every collector of Sussex books will have his own ideas about which books are local classics and their opinions will differ. There are, nonetheless, a small number of books that you might expect to find in any significant collection. These are books like *The Spirit of the Downs* by Arthur Beckett, *The Shepherds of Sussex* by Barclay Wills and *A Dictionary of the Sussex Dialect* by the Rev. W.D. Parish; books that have stood the test of time without losing any of their appeal.

This volume provides biographical sketches of the authors of these works, highlighting how they were connected with the county. Some of the writers were, as one might expect, born and bred in Sussex, but some came to the county as children, some came later in life and one was only ever a visitor. Some were concerned to record a local way of life that was disappearing and some sought to uncover the past, while others simply celebrated their emotional attachment to the county by trying to explain what made it so special for them. All gave their work a personal stamp, an originality that sets it apart from run of the mill county guides and memoirs.

Selecting the writers has not been easy but a line had to drawn somewhere. The only rule I imposed on myself was that I would exclude living authors. Otherwise, the choice can only be attributed to my idiosyncratic judgement.

Richard Knowles

ARTHUR BECKETT

The Spirit of the Downs, 1909

The Wonderful Weald, 1911

Adventures of a Quiet Man, 1933

Arthur Beckett was a successful journalist, newspaper proprietor, author and environmental campaigner. He characterised himself as a 'quiet man' but he exercised considerable influence. Through his books and the Sussex County Magazine, which he founded and edited, he stimulated widespread interest in Sussex, and in his capacity as president of the Society of Sussex Downsmen he helped to prevent several developments that would have scarred the South Downs irrevocably.

He was born in Yorkshire but grew up in Eastbourne after his father, T.R. Beckett, moved there to take over the *Eastbourne Gazette*. He attended private schools in the town completing his education at New College, when the headmaster was still its founder, Frederick Schreiner, brother of the novelist, Olive Schreiner.

He enjoyed a long career in journalism, editing local papers and magazines. Latterly he was Chairman and Governing Director of T.R. Beckett Ltd., newspaper proprietors of Eastbourne, Lewes, Worthing and London.

As a journalist he contributed to many national newspapers and magazines including *The Times*, the *Morning Post*, the *Spectator*, *Country Life* and *The Field*. Over the years he wrote on many topics but his favourite subject was always Sussex; his first article about the county having appeared in the *Gentleman's Magazine* in 1898. His knowledge of Sussex was encyclopaedic and he packed a wealth of Sussex lore into his two most successful books, *The Spirit of the Downs* and *The Wonderful Weald*.

Beckett's stated intention was that *The Spirit of the Downs* should be a discursive book and after some introductory chapters he takes us on a journey from South Harting to Beachy Head evoking the character of each locality along his route by relating anecdotes, recalling history and describing landscape. As a literary device he takes a companion, 'Amicus', his alter ego, and this enables him to maintain a conversational style. The book is packed with downland lore and should be read by everyone who loves the South Downs. *The Spirit of the Downs* was first published in 1909 with twenty colour plates from paintings by Stanley Inchbold, later editions are illustrated with twelve photographs and the text of the fifth was revised with the help of Dr E. Cecil Curwen to take account of the latest archaeological discoveries.

The Wonderful Weald follows a similar format but the author's companion on this perambulation is 'Aminta', a literary incarnation of his wife, Alice. 'Aminta' also features in *The Adventures of a Quiet Man*, Beckett's last and least satisfactory book, which first appeared serially in the *Sussex County Magazine* during 1930.

Beckett also wrote a novel, several poems and the libretto for an opera. His novel, *Emancipation*, was published in 1907 and ran to eight editions, a collection of poems, *Sussex at War and Poems of Peace*, appeared in 1916, and the opera, *Dacre of the South*, with music by J.R. Dear, was performed by the Eastbourne Amateur Operatic and Dramatic Society in 1926.

Beckett was a leading light in the Society of Sussex Downsmen but it was his friend, Robert Thurston Hopkins, who first floated the idea of forming the Society. Hopkin's objective was that the Society should stimulate an appreciation of the South Downs and campaign vigorously to protect the hills from indiscriminate building. He was overwhelmed by the public interest in his proposal and organised an inaugural meeting at the Royal Pavilion, Brighton. He had, however, no intention of speaking in public. Having already ensured that Arthur Beckett would attend he led him to the platform by subterfuge and then, when the right moment, came "poked him vigorously." As Hopkins had hoped, Beckett took charge of the proceedings and was elected to be their president. He was a fortunate choice for although he claimed to be a quiet man he was a determined and doughty fighter; just the man they needed to lead their opposition to the speculative building syndicates that were formulating proposals for downland developments.

The growth of Peacehaven had already shown what damage could be done when speculators were given free rein. Happily, the Downsmen prevented many other potential atrocities. In 1925 a proposal to build bungalows near the Devil's Dyke was dropped in response to objections raised jointly by the Downsmen and the Commons and Footpaths Preservation Society. The Downsmen were in action again in 1926 when a building syndicate secured an option on a 480-acre site that included a stretch of the Seven Sisters. The syndicate named a price for abandoning its project and, eventually, through appeals initiated by the Downsmen and some very generous individual donations, the site was bought and saved. The Downsmen also intervened, twice, to prevent a motor-racing track being constructed on the northern escarpment of the Downs above Edburton. In these instances and many others Beckett played a leading part. As A.H. Anderson, chairman of the Downsmen's Planning Committee, reported in 1936, "Mr Arthur Beckett, so far from regarding his office as ornamental or honorary, has never ceased to throw all his weight and influence into the fight. He has, in particular, represented the Society at numerous public enquiries and on deputations before the House of Lords, the Prime Minister, and locally." All of us who appreciate the South Downs owe a debt of gratitude to Arthur Beckett.

When Beckett founded the *Sussex County Magazine* in 1926 he knew that he was responding to a growing interest in the county among both natives and newcomers. Literary and photographic material flowed in during its first year and sales grew steadily both at home and abroad. Issues were initially priced at sixpence but Beckett had ambitions to increase the size of the magazine and recognised that the price would have to rise. He bided his time and then gave his readers a choice by enclosing a voting slip and a stamped addressed envelope with each copy of the October 1928 issue. He could, he explained, maintain the price at sixpence by printing on cheaper paper and reducing the number of illustrations. Alternatively he could increase the price to a shilling and print more pages. As he had hoped ninety percent of his respondents opted for the increase.

The magazine then settled into a regular format and went from strength to strength. 'A Countryman's Diary' by A.A. Evans and 'Historic Houses of Sussex' by Viscountess Wolseley became regular features and a number of books including *Shepherds of Sussex* by Barclay Wills and *A Southdown Farm in the Sixties* by Maude Robinson were first printed serially in its pages.

Year by year subscribers were able to have their copies of the magazine bound in blue cloth with gilt lettering and the volumes built up to form a vast repository of Sussex topography, archaeology, history and folklore. Many contributions were of a high academic standard and every issue was lavishly illustrated. I find the thirty volumes a continual source of pleasure and would recommend anyone who has them to keep an eye out for the comprehensive index that was produced by Hove Library in 1966.

In 1940 the size of the magazine was reduced to conform to wartime economies but the hardest blow came with the death of its founder and editor in 1943. Arthur Beckett had, as his brother put it, "delighted in editing the *Sussex County Magazine*" and those who knew him called it 'his baby'.

Arthur Beckett died on 8th May 1943, after a long and painful illness. He was cremated at Brighton and his ashes were buried in the churchyard of Friston, where his wife had been laid to rest in 1938. His grave is therefore in the downland that he loved so much and fought so hard to protect. Fellow author and journalist, George Aitchison, paid tribute in verse to the way Beckett had loved and served his county. The following is the final couplet.

> Guard still, O watchman, Sussex fields and towns,
> Quiet man, warrior, Spirit of the Downs.

The *Sussex County Magazine* survived his death but began to lose money during the years of austerity that followed the Second World War. By 1956 the losses had reached £1,000 a year and the editorial staff announced that the July issue would be the last. It had been an outstanding magazine and on 13th April the prospect of its demise was noted with some solemnity in the columns of *The Times*. "As the last issue leaves the printer, it will seem to some of us as if a familiar piece of English downland, a vast block of Regency granite on Brighton's front, or even the Seven Sisters, had suddenly tumbled into the sea."

The final issue included a dialect poem by W.G. Daish, which ended with the following stanza.

> Still, Sussex folks can count dur blessins yet
> En one thing sartinsure afore dey start,
> Whur in but in dese volumes should us git
> A fitter srine fur o'd Mus' Beckett's heart!

HILAIRE BELLOC

Sussex, Painted by Wilfrid Ball, 1906.

The Four Men, 1912.

The County of Sussex, 1936.

It was during his boyhood at Slindon that Hilaire Belloc developed his love of Sussex and his feelings only deepened, as he grew older. They were probably best expressed in his verse, particularly in *The South Country* and *Duncton Hill* but they are also reflected in some inspired essays and a minor masterpiece, *The Four Men*.

Hilaire Belloc was, like Dr. Johnson, a prolific writer who is now better remembered for his boisterous personality than for his books. Also, again like Dr. Johnson, he held dogmatic views on most subjects, and could be relied upon to argue his case with absolute conviction. He dominated by sheer force of personality. He was larger than life.

Belloc was satisfied with very few of the books that he wrote and admitted that most of them were dashed off as money-spinners. Most of his histories and biographies fall into this category and his attitude to them is illustrated by an incident that took place in a railway carriage during the 1930s. Belloc observed that the man sitting opposite to him was reading one of his books and asked him what it had cost. Belloc then refunded him the money, snatched the book and threw it out of the window declaring that it was rubbish! The story may be apocryphal but it is just the sort

Belloc in 1932
after a drawing by Daphne Pollen

of thing that he would have done!

Hilaire Belloc was born at La Celle Saint Cloud, near Paris, in July 1870, to a French father, Louis Belloc, and an English mother, Bessie (Parkes). He was born only days before the outbreak of the Franco-Prussian War and the family decided that Bessie should immediately leave for England taking Hilaire and his sister so that they should escape the dangers of the conflict. When they returned to France in June 1871 they found that their home had been wantonly vandalised by the Prussian troops. It took weeks of work to make it habitable but even then their troubles were not at an end. In August 1872 Louis Belloc died unexpectedly. Bessie was devastated but he left her comfortably off and for some years she was able to divide her time between La Celle Saint Cloud and London. This arrangement continued until 1878, when her financial position suddenly worsened as a consequence of the imprudence of her stockbroker. She then found it necessary to sell the lease of the London house and decided to settle at Slindon in Sussex where they could live more cheaply. Young Belloc loved the area and, perhaps because he was experiencing a sense of permanence and stability for the first time, it took on a significance that would stay with him for the rest of his life.

He was educated at the Oratory school in Edgbaston under Cardinal Newman, and then, after an interval of three years, at Balliol College, Oxford. At Oxford he established a formidable reputation as a speaker in the debates of the Oxford Union and in due course became its President. He graduated with first class honours in History and his career as a writer began immediately with the publication of *Verses and Sonnets* in 1895. *The Bad Child's Book of Beasts* followed in 1896. At one stage it appeared that he might enter his father's profession and become a lawyer; then politics seemed more likely and from 1906 to 1910 he was the Liberal M.P. for South Salford. It was, however, mainly through his writing that he earned his living.

He married Elodie Hogan, an American, in 1896 and after living for spells in London and Oxford they returned to Slindon in 1905 with their growing family. They lived at Court Hill farm for eighteen months and then moved to Shipley where, for just £900 he purchased the freehold of five acres with a rambling brick house and a picturesque working windmill. This was 'King's Land' which remained his home until he died in 1953. The house had no water supply but at a cost of just £100 he was able to add a well, pump, cistern and WCs. The house also lacked such conveniences as a bathroom, electricity and gas and he resisted the introduction of these innovations for many years!

Belloc loved Sussex and called it England's Eden – 'that centre of all good things and home of happy men'. Some of his best prose was written in praise of the county and is to be found in his essays. *The Mowing of a Field* in the collection entitled *Hills and the Sea* (1906) is one of his finest achievements. Other essays about the county in the same book are *The Valley of the Rother* and, reflecting his love of sailing, *The Slant of the Land*, which describes a sailor's view of the Sussex coast.

Belloc was less successful when he wrote a description of the physical nature and historical development of the county for a lavishly illustrated book entitled *Sussex Painted by Wilfrid Ball* (1906). The text was secondary to the 75 colour plates and his authorship was not acknowledged but many readers recognised his style. Some decades later Belloc extensively revised and expanded the text for publication as *The County of Sussex* (1936) but even this version is disappointing!

Belloc's Sussex masterpiece is *The Four Men* (1912). The four men of the title are the narrator and three companions who join him as he rambles across the county; the latter are 'Grizzlebeard', a cynical grey-haired philosopher, 'Sailor', a restless much travelled mariner, and 'Poet', an inspired but unworldly scribbler. It is an eccentric book that is difficult to categorise. It could be classified as a picaresque novel with characters that personify facets of the author's personality. I have also seen it listed under 'travel' because it chronicles a journey, but that is far too simplistic. Belloc called it a 'farrago' and it is probably best to settle for his description!

The Four Men is a book that people either love or hate. If you consult *Sussex Cottage* (1936) by Esther Meynell you will find that she considered it to be the most perfect book ever written on Sussex, whereas in *Along the South Downs* (1958) you will learn that David Harrison found it almost unreadable! Harrison does, however, go on to say that he supposes that it must have some esoteric significance!

The book chronicles how, in 1902, four men walked from the 'George' inn at Robertsbridge, near the Sussex border with Kent, across the county to South Harting near the border with Hampshire. As they tramp westward they talk, tales are told, philosophy is expounded, countryside is described, inns are visited, songs are sung, spurious history is recalled and poetry is composed. We learn how Squire Fuller of Brightling gave a eulogy upon the county of Sussex to the House of Commons, how St Dunstan pulled the devil by his nose at Mayfield, why Washington ale is so good, how the men of Sussex defeated the men of Kent in the great Battle of Battle, what Mr. Justice Honeybubble had to say in the 'Cricketer's Arms' at Duncton, and much more. The book concludes with Belloc's most moving poem – *Duncton Hill*. Truly this book is pure Sussex.

The book is also an exploration of Belloc himself and its import, expressed so beautifully in the closing poem, is that any man's immortality is bound up with the land he has known and loved. It is certainly an unusual book and could only have been written by an eccentric, opinionated genius like Hilaire Belloc. Belloc's biographer, A.N. Wilson describes it as a prose elegy.

Recently another notable Sussex character, Bob Copper, retraced the steps of the four men and recorded his experience in *Across Sussex with Belloc* (1994). He had expected to find Sussex much altered but his comforting conclusion was that it had changed less than the casual observer would expect. That conclusion would have surprised Belloc who believed that the Sussex he knew and loved was doomed and that it would not long survive him.

I cannot now do better than finish by quoting Esther Meynell's opinion of this book more fully. Her comments come from a chapter on Sussex books in *Sussex Cottage*. "Good and indispensable are all these books, and many others, but there is a book called *The Four Men* which holds a place held by no other, as it is the most perfect book that has ever been written on Sussex. It is not only about Sussex, but is the complete expression of a personality that has so linked itself with the county – that of Mr. Hilaire Belloc. And it is a book that is an ideal companion, either when in Sussex to make one realise the quality of that privilege, or when out of Sussex to assuage the inevitable nostalgia."

NATHANIEL PAYNE BLAKER

Sussex in Bygone Days, 1919.

Nathaniel Blaker was an eminent surgeon and when Dr Newsholme suggested that he should write down his recollections Newsholme had expected that they would throw light on the remarkable advances in medical science that had taken place over the preceding half-century. Instead, when Blaker put pen to paper, he became absorbed with memories of life in the village where he grew up and this contributed more than two thirds of his memoir!

Nathaniel Payne Blaker was born in 1835, on the farm of his maternal grandfather in the parish of Selmeston. His father, Nathaniel Blaker, was also a farmer and came from a family that had owned land around Portslade, Kingston and Shoreham for centuries. His parents moved to Perching Manor Farm in Edburton before his first birthday and he grew up there. Early in his memoir he gives us a picture of the parish with its hamlet of Fulking, as it was when he was a boy.

Perching Manor Farm

"The population was almost entirely composed of agricultural labourers and their families, with the village shopkeeper, the publican and one or two market gardeners. These labourers were a strong and hardy set of men, industrious, truthful and honest, with very few exceptions. Their dress was usually a dark smock frock, with elaborate pleating at the shoulders, knee breeches, leather gaiters and laced boots. On Sunday they wore a scrupulously white smock frock. Their food consisted of bread and cheese, vegetables, bacon and pudding, with fresh meat only occasionally. The roads at this time were very narrow, rough and muddy, and locomotion was very slow and difficult, consequently they rarely travelled far from home, some never going out of their own parish; indeed, it was a common saying that Sussex girls had such long legs because they stretched them by pulling them out of the mud in the roads."

Blaker's reminiscences cover every aspect of local agricultural life and his book has chapters on such topics as 'Ox-teams', 'Sheep Washing', 'Sheep Shearing', 'Haying', 'Harvest' and 'Hollering Pot.' Each provides a masterly picture of bygone life, sharply observed and simply told.

Blaker learnt the rudiments of reading, writing and arithmetic from his mother before going to the school of Miss Lee at Lewes, when he was eight. After a year he moved to the Grammar School where he considered that he was well looked after and well educated. He left school at sixteen and then spent a year back at Edburton, learning farming. Looking back he believed that it had been the best possible preparation for his education as a surgeon and declared that his treatment of patients had sometimes been modified to their advantage by what he had learned from watching animals and their management!

In June 1852 he enrolled as a pupil at the Sussex County Hospital and after a probationary month was articled to the House Surgeon for five years with an understanding that he would be permitted to spend the last two years at a London teaching hospital. In those days the wards at the County Hospital had plain whitewashed walls and bare wooden floors, the beds were close together and, as the windows were generally kept closed, he found the smell sickening. In 1855 he entered Guy's Hospital in London and spent the first winter session mainly in the dissecting room. While he was at Guy's he grew friendly with a medical student at St Bartholomew's and on one evening they went to an Italian opera. They were unimpressed. "So far from enjoying it" he wrote, "I am afraid we compared it to some lunatics dressed up and jumping about the stage screaming at the top of their voices. I recollect, also, we left and consoled ourselves with an oyster supper."

Before he had completed his time at Guy's he fell ill and had to return home, apparently in the last stages of phthisis (probably tuberculosis). He slowly recovered and although he was not able to return to Guy's he found that he had completed sufficient time in recognised hospitals to be allowed to take to take his exams, which he did in 1858.

A month after qualifying he received a letter from the Sussex County Hospital to say that their newly appointed House Surgeon had scarlet fever and asking if he could take over. He did so and stayed for three months. He then went to Guy's for some months before being appointed assistant surgeon at the Convict Hospital, which was then being housed temporarily at Lewes, but was afterwards transferred to new premises at Knapp Hill near Woking.

In 1860 he was appointed House Surgeon to the Brighton and Hove Dispensary and was there through local epidemics of diphtheria, smallpox and scarlet fever. The latter was the most serious and he could remember signing 23 death certificates in just one month. He attributed the spread of both the diphtheria and scarlet fever epidemics to primitive drainage. In the areas of Brighton that were most seriously affected the drains fed into cesspits that had been sunk into the chalk and were rarely if ever emptied because the contents invariably seeped away.

He left the Dispensary in 1862 and in 1864 was elected House Surgeon to the Sussex County Hospital, a post he had wanted ever since his days there as a pupil. He found that the morbid fear of fresh air still prevailed but ventilation was improved soon after his return. He also comments that it was at this time that the clinical thermometer and hypodermic syringe came into use. At the end of 1867 he left and in 1869 was appointed Assistant Surgeon. Although he worked in Brighton he often got away and loved riding in the countryside. He found the sense of freedom exhilarating by day but observed that a ride on a fine summer night was even more enjoyable.

"Horses always went well at night and seldom shied or stumbled, and to walk along with the rein loose on his neck in those lanes, overshadowed by trees, with all nature at rest, the stillness only broken by the flight and note of a night bird, the barking of a fox in the woods, the tinkling of a sheep-bell or some other occasional country sound, was almost heavenly."

If that extract from Blaker's reminiscences appears idyllic the following picture of a Brighton slum will provide a grim contrast. It describes two alleys that opened into North Road, then called North Lane. They were on the site of what is now Tichbourne Street.

"As far as I recollect the houses were mere huts with a few feet of garden in front, and in a most dilapidated condition. The inhabitants, mostly fishermen were of the lowest type; the families lived all crowded together, and I have seen on Sunday mornings girls of ten or twelve years old, or even a year or two older, walking in front of the houses absolutely naked. In the gardens and paths in front of the houses, heads skins and intestines of fish were lying about in every stage of decomposition. Nothing could be worse than the sanitary conditions, and yet there was a remarkable freedom from illness, though Bread Street above and Gardner Street below had their full share."

In 1869 he married Fanny Jane Smith and moved into 29, Old Steine. The house was connected to a brick drain that ran down to the sea but the smell emanating from its gully holes was sometimes very noticeable and large black slugs used to come up through cracks into the basement; a situation that persisted until the local drains were improved in 1871.

Blaker became a well-known figure in and around Brighton. E.V. Lucas often saw him doing his rounds in his phaeton and described him as "a thin, spare man, clean shaven with an odd crooked face and piercing eyes with a sideways look." Dr Habberton Lulham, who, as a young man had acted as his 'dresser' at the Sussex County Hospital remembered him for his professionalism and general kindliness of manner.

When he retired Blaker moved to 'Cherington', Hurstpierpoint, and it was there that he wrote his reminiscences. The memoir was first published for private circulation in 1906 and then largely rewritten for a wider public in 1919. In 1906 he ended on a note of despair at what he perceived to be a general disintegration of character and softening of manly fibre. He was, however, reassured when he saw how the country faced the challenges of the First World War and the 1919 edition of his memoir ends with him hoping that the nation will retain the simple Spartan virtues that he had feared were being lost

He died in 1920 and his kindliness was apparent in his will for he left annuities to some of his servants and made generous bequests to others.

E. Cecil Curwen

Prehistoric Sussex, 1929

The Archaeology of Sussex, 1954.

Dr E. Cecil Curwen could always remember when his interest in archaeology was kindled. He was about seven years old at the time and had accompanied his father, Dr Eliot Curwen, on a ramble from Southwick over Thundersbarrow Hill to the Devil's Dyke. "The day was dull" he recalled, " and the sky was heavy with leaden clouds under which the grey-green hills lay in gloomy silence. The very name of Thundersbarrow Hill, especially on such a day, sounded awesome and grand. On its back the vague outlines of a 'camp', marked on the map, were pointed out, and thereafter the way was beguiled with tales of ancient gods and heroes, till on our arrival at the Dyke the storm broke in full fury, the thunder crashing and roaring and echoing round the heavens, as if old Thunor himself were pursuing the wanderers from his sacred hill. The effect on a child's mind can readily be understood."

Young Cecil Curwen was hooked and he would never again look at the beauty of the South Downs without wanting to interpret its earthworks and dig through the turf in order to discover more about the ancient peoples who once lived there. He would also write about them and the passage that I have quoted demonstrates Curwen's ability to paint a vivid picture in words. It was a gift that marked him out from many other archaeologists and made his findings available to a wide readership.

Eliot Cecil Curwen was born in 1895, in Peking (now Beijing), China, where his father was working as a medical missionary. Following their return to England the family settled in Hove where Dr Eliot Curwen remained in general practice for fifty years. Cecil Curwen was educated at Rugby and Gonville and Caius College, Cambridge, before attending St Thomas' Hospital where he trained for the medical profession, qualifying in 1921.

Although both father and son were in general practice they found time to undertake an immense workload in the field of archaeology and often worked together. Their approach to every project was methodical and their reports were exemplary for their clarity. They were the most professional of amateur archaeologists and their teams included a number of the young men, like Stuart Piggott and Grahame Clark, who went on to enjoy distinguished careers in archaeology.

The Curwens' excavation of the Iron Age hill fort on the Caburn, near Lewes, is a typical example of their work. They conducted the dig jointly over four months commencing in October 1925 with just one assistant, one labourer and a few occasional helpers. The work enabled them to draw definitive conclusions and these were reported in the *Sussex Archaeological Collections* (Volume LXVIII, 1927, pp.1-56).

Three of the most important excavations that Cecil Curwen led personally were conducted at Whitehawk, on Brighton Racecourse, in 1929, 1932-3 and 1935. His work revealed a vivid picture of a primitive Neolithic community whose people disposed of their dead without, as Curwen put it, "any token of care or esteem." Some of the other important excavations he supervised were conducted in 1928 and 1930, at the Neolithic and Iron Age sites on the Trundle, four miles north of Chichester, and in 1934, at a Bronze Age site at Plumpton Plain, northwest of Lewes, where he worked jointly with G.A. Holleyman.

G.P. Burstow who taught at Brighton College, often assisted Cecil Curwen and a journal recording his part in the excavation of Thundersbarrow in the spring of 1932 was published in the *Sussex County Magazine* in July 1942. He describes, among other things, a visit to the doctor's house at 34 Medina Villas, Hove, where he was ushered into Curwen's 'archaeological room'. It had large-scale maps of the south coast round the walls and finds from Thundersbarrow were spread across

E Cecil Curwen in 1927

a table at one end.

Cecil Curwen was the author of numerous reports that were published in professional journals but he also contributed to the *Sussex County Magazine*. His lengthy article, *Sussex from the Air*, is an example, which appeared serially from July 1930 to March 1931, and demonstrated what a valuable tool air-photography had become for the interpretation of earthworks. He also wrote five books, two of which deserve a place in any collection of Sussex books. They are *Prehistoric Sussex* and *The Archaeology of Sussex*. In the first the material is organised by type of site with chapter headings like 'The Flint Mines' and 'The Hill-Forts'. In the second the arrangement is chronological taking us from the earliest times to the end of the Roman period. Both books are admirable but the latter has the advantage of having been published in 1954, a quarter of a century after the first; enabling the author to take account of a great many important excavations that had been conducted in the interim.

When Cecil Curwen was awarded an O.B.E. in the 1955 New Years Honours nobody should have been surprised, but it was not awarded for his services to archaeology, it was in recognition of his having been Honorary Physician to the Police Convalescent Seaside Home on Portland Road, Hove!

He lived in Hove for most of his life at 1 St Aubyns, 34 Medina Villas and 95 Goldstone Crescent but moved to Eastbourne in 1962 and died there a few years later. The Sussex Archaeological Society marked his passing with an obituary in *Sussex Notes and Queries* paying tribute to him in unequivocal terms. "In the field of Sussex Prehistoric Archaeology he was far and away our most outstanding member."

HOWARD DUDLEY

Juvenile Researches, 1835

The History and Antiquities of Horsham, 1836

Howard Dudley was a precocious young man who published two works about Sussex before he was seventeen. He was born in London on 13th March 1820, the son of George Dudley, formerly of Tipperary, and his wife Sarah, the daughter of a London coal merchant. His parents were Quakers but he was baptised at St Leonard's church in Shoreditch. According to his obituary in the *Gentleman's Magazine* this was done surreptitiously "through the zeal of his nurse."

Following the death of his father, at Ghent in 1827, his mother moved to Easebourne, near Midhurst, where Howard and his sister were enchanted with the Sussex countryside through which they rode and rambled. Both were observant, both enjoyed drawing what they saw and both could write verse but Howard decided to go further. Shortly before his fifteenth birthday he produced a small book about the area in which he described Chichester, Midhurst, Easebourne, Petersfield, Petworth and Horsham. He made wood engravings of his drawings for the illustrations, set the type and printed it page by page on his own hand press. The volume measuring just 4 inches by 5, comprised 130 pages and was entitled *Juvenile Researches, or a Description of some of the principal Towns of the Western part of Sussex, and the borders of Hants. Interspersed with various pieces of Poetry, by a Sister: and illustrated by numerous wood-engravings, executed by the Author. The whole being composed and printed by a boy of 14.*

The small book had its faults but proved so popular with Howard's relations, friends and acquaintances that he produced a second, expanded edition. This was also printed in 1835, but after his birthday, and the new title page acknowledged his authorship with the words "Printed and composed by H. Dudley aged 15."

Shortly after this the family returned to London, to Millbank Street,

Westminster, where young Dudley produced his next work, *The History and Antiquities of Horsham*. The new book, which measured 7½ inches by 5, was illustrated with 30 wood engravings and four lithographic views. It was dedicated to the Earl of Egremont, "with his lordship's permission" and this aristocratic encouragement suggests that the earl must have seen and been impressed by a copy of *Juvenile Researches*, in which his seat at Petworth was described.

The History and Antiquities of Horsham provides a concise description of the town, its buildings and the neighbouring countryside along with relevant historical information. The illustrations vary in quality but most of them are charming and some are excellent. A few provide views of buildings which, like the Horsham Gaol, have since been demolished. At the end of the book he quotes from a survey of the county dating from 1730 and mentions that it is in the possession of Miss Cove of Albion Terrace. The lady was undoubtedly a relation of his mother, probably her sister, and it may have been while staying with her that his interest in Horsham was aroused. Dudley left no record of how many copies of the book he had printed but the number must have been small for printing on his hand press would have been an exceedingly laborious process. Of those that were printed only a few have survived.

Dudley later issued a prospectus for a more ambitious quarto volume, *The History and Antiquities of Midhurst and its Vicinity*, which he proposed to illustrate with more than 150 wood engravings and lithographic drawings. Unfortunately, the project was never completed. Dudley had become a professional wood-engraver and his commissions doubtless filled his time.

Between 1845 and 1852 he lived in Edinburgh and while he was there married Jane Ellen Young, whose brothers, Charles and Alexander, were also engravers. When Dudley returned to London he settled in Holford Square, Pentonville, where he was known as a mild and amiable man with a strong religious faith.

He died at his home in 1864, aged only 44, and, although he had been a professional wood-engraver for many years, it is for his juvenile work that he is remembered. Even his obituary in the *Gentleman's Magazine* (January 1865) describes little other than his Sussex books.

Very few copies of Dudley's books have survived but facsimile editions of his *History and Antiquities of Horsham* have been published, by Jury Cramp in 1973, and by Country Books in 2002.

* * *

In the year that Howard Dudley died another remarkable Horsham historian, William Albery, was born. He was a saddler and harness maker who inherited a family business that had been founded in 1810, and later gained the distinction of being elected president of the Federation of Master Saddlers of Great Britain. He was a man of many parts with a passionate interest in music and local history. He played the cornet, was one of the founders of the Horsham Borough Silver Band and was a prime mover in the campaign that resulted in the establishment of a town museum.

His first book came about because he was encouraged to record the recollections of another local craftsman, Henry Burstow (1824-1916), a boot-and-shoemaker who was more widely known as a campanologist and singer of folk songs. Burstow had a repertoire of over 400 traditional songs and his reputation attracted a visit by Vaughan Williams who recorded his singing on a phonograph. Albery only expected the old man's memories to provide sufficient material for a pamphlet but they were so rich, varied and extensive that the result was a book. It was published in 1911 with the title – *Reminiscences of Horsham, Being Recollections of Henry Burstow, the Celebrated Bell-ringer and Song Singer, with Some Account of the Old Bell Foundry at Horsham, of the Horsham Parish Church Bells and of Famous Peals Rung by Horsham Ringers, Together with a List of the 400 and Odd Songs He Sings from Memory.*

Albery's next work was a carefully researched *Parliamentary History of Horsham*, which was published in 1927 with an introduction by Hilaire Belloc. Over the years that followed he made a number of contributions to the Sussex County Magazine, the most substantial being 'The Sussex County Gaol at Horsham' (1540-1845), which appeared from May to December 1932 and 'Sussex Smugglers', which appeared from July to December 1934. His final work, a substantial volume entitled *A Millennium of Facts in the History of Horsham and Sussex*, was issued in 1947, just three years before he died.

TICKNER EDWARDES

The Bee Master of Warrilow, 1906.
An Idler in the Wilds, 1906.
Neighbourhood, 1911.
A Downland Year, 1939.

Tickner Edwardes was born and brought up in London but he had no inclination to follow in his father's footsteps by becoming a businessman. He chose instead to live in a cottage in the village of Burpham, near Arundel. There he turned his hand to bee keeping and journalism, contributing regular articles on country life to a number of magazines. His first book *Sidelights of Nature*, was a collection of essays published in 1898. Another early book, also a collection of essays, was *An Idler in the Wilds* (1906) and I suspect that its title reveals exactly how he saw himself at that stage in his life!

The most popular books that he wrote were *The Bee Master of Warrilow* (1906) and *The Lore of the Honey Bee* (1908) which are both bee-keeping classics. The first edition of the former is a slim volume but a revised and enlarged edition was published in 1920 and has been re-issued as recently as 1983. 'Warrilow' is described as a precipitous little village tucked away under the green brink of the South Downs and is, of course, Burpham, where Edwardes lived and kept his bees. *The Lore of the Honey Bee* was a more ambitious work covering the history and mythology of bee-keeping from the earliest times. It ran to many editions and its merits led his publishers to suggest the he might write a bee-keeping novel. He did so and when *The Honey Star* was published in 1913 it was well received by the book critic on the Evening Standard who reported that Tickner Edwardes had done for Sussex much what Thomas Hardy had done for Wessex. This was, however, pure hyperbole! The plot and the characters are unconvincing and the public were not impressed. It did not sell in large numbers and is now very rare indeed.

Edwardes was keen to make his name as a novelist but this did not stem the flow of his non-fiction. *Lift Luck on Southern Roads* was published in 1910 and *Neighbourhood* followed in 1911. The former is an account of a hitchhiking journey and the Sussex content is limited. *Neighbourhood*, on the other hand, is set entirely in a Sussex village. Edwardes calls the place 'Windlecombe' but his book provides a thinly disguised portrait of Burpham. It lies, he explains, "just where the Arun river breaks the green rampart of the Sussex Downs" and its greatest blessing is its isolation, for there is no road through the village. The road leading to it reaches all of its houses but then "changes to a mere cart-track, soon to vanish altogether in the green sward of the Downs."

In *Neighbourhood* he describes life in the village month by month, chronicling the changing seasons. He describes farming, flora and fauna, and we are introduced to several local characters. We meet a downland shepherd George Artlett, old Miss Angel who keeps the 'sweetstuff' shop and Tom Clemmer, the smith, who is "of the old South Saxon blood" and all of them are brought to life by his pen. In the June chapter Edwardes is lyrical describing the annual sheep-wash " and in the next he captures the atmosphere of a rural cricket match. *Neighbourhood* provides us with a truly engaging glimpse of life in a downland village at the beginning of the twentieth century. It is book to be treasured and reread, a Sussex classic.

Neighbourhood also reveals something of the author's own philosophy of life. We learn that his attendance at church was irregular. "For" he explains, "there never was human man, whether lay or clerical, who, of a fine Sunday morning, believed himself so nearly at one with his Maker on his knees in a dusty pew, as abroad in the vast green church of an English country-side." I wonder if his views changed when, many years later, he became the vicar of Burpham! I doubt it. He simply loved walking, especially on the Downs and his words are sheer prose poetry when he describes his feelings for the Downs. "Somehow or other, every stride upward over the springy turf seems to lighten the load; and once on the summit, you seem to have lifted head and shoulders far above the strife. The hurrying mountain freshet of a breeze singing in your ears, and the rippling lark-music, have washed the heart clean of all but gladness, and you see with awakened eyes".

We are indebted to another writer, John Cowper Powys, who moved to Burpham in 1902, for a vivid picture of Edwardes at that time. The two men became friends and Powys later recalled that there had been a tough-wood texture to the physical presence of the shy beekeeper. He also wrote of his essential goodness, his gravity and his imperturbable reserve. Edwardes was then living in a plain red brick house that was appropriately known as the Red Cottage; but Powys tells us that a smaller cottage nearby was his literary retreat. There he laboured over his manuscripts, weighing up each choice of words with the infinite care of a true craftsman.

Neighbourhood was followed by Edwardes' second novel, *Tansy* (1914), and that proved to be his best and most successful work of fiction. *Tansy*, is a tale of shepherding on the South Downs and its formidable heroine, Tansy Firle, is an attractive young woman who becomes the shepherdess at Fair Mile Farm after the untimely death of her father. The farmer's sons, both fall for her and developments are further complicated when her former lover, the dissolute foreman of a gang of steam-threshers, arrives on the scene. Highpoints of the shepherding year are skilfully incorporated into the narrative and are vividly described. *Tansy* could have been set almost anywhere along the length of the South Downs but it was Burpham that Edwardes had in mind, and Peppering Farm, a little to the north of the village, was the prototype for Fair Mile Farm.

His writing was interrupted by the outbreak of the First World War when, although he was nearly fifty years old, he enlisted as a private in the R.A.M.C. and saw action at Gallipoli. By 1917 he had risen to be a Staff Sergeant-Major and was attached to the G.H.Q. of the Egyptian Expeditionary Force. He was commissioned in 1918 and promoted to Captain in January 1919, just before completing his military service as a medical entomologist on the staff of Colonel Sir Ronald Ross, malaria consultant to the War Office.

His wartime experiences strengthened his religious faith and after returning to civilian life he went to theological college. In 1920 he was ordained to the curacy of Lyminster, near Arundel, remaining there until 1925 when he appointed Rector of Folkington. Then, in 1927, he became Vicar of Burpham and returned to the village where he had lived for so many years before taking Holy Orders.

After his ordination he wrote three more novels, *The Seventh Wave* (1922), *Sunset Bride* (1927) and *Eve the Enemy* (1931) all with Sussex villages settings. Unfortunately, none of them are the equal of *Tansy*, which was filmed for the silent screen in 1929 with Alma Taylor in the title role.

Edwardes also continued to write about nature in the Sussex countryside producing *A Country Calendar* (1928) and *A Downland Year* (1939), which demonstrated that his powers of observation and his ability to write evocative prose were undiminished.

Despite his distinguished war record and his continuing success as a writer Edwardes remained a modest, mild-mannered man who was happiest living in the heart of the West Sussex countryside where he and his wife never tired of walking. He resigned his living in 1935 but remained in the village and died there at the end of 1944.

After his death one of his friends described him as 'Nature's Essayist' but he had been known locally as 'the bee-man of Burpham' and that is probably how he would have liked to be remembered.

J. COKER EGERTON

Sussex Folk and Sussex Ways, 1884.

When Robert Thurston Hopkins was in Burwash doing research for a book about Kipling he visited the Bell Inn and met the Sexton of the village church, who had called in for a pint. The man was old enough to have known the Rev. Egerton and Thurston Hopkins recorded the following recollection of choir practice in the 1870s when the Sexton might well have been one of the choir' boys.

"He had a hem o' trouble with the boys," the old man drawled, "and the only way he could make 'em behave reasonable like was to crack' em on the head with his fiddle stick. He was odd-fashioned, no bounds, was the old rector."

John Coker Egerton was born in Cheshire in 1829, son of the Rev. John Egerton, of Bunbury, who resigned his living in 1849, when he was only 52 years old, and retired to a family property at Hextable, Kent. Young Egerton was educated at Shrewsbury and Brasenose, Oxford where he rowed for his college. After graduating he was ordained and became curate at Nunton, near Salisbury. Then, in 1857, he was invited to become curate at Burwash in East Sussex where his uncle, the Rev. John Gould was rector and owner of the advowson. With the exception of three years at St Andrew's Undershaft in the City of London, from 1862 to 1865, he remained at Burwash until he succeeded his uncle as rector in 1867. Egerton eventually spent the best part of thirty years in Burwash but he never lost touch with the rowing fraternity at Oxford or his former parishioners at Nunton.

His diary suggests that he was a diligent parish priest but he reviewed his life ruefully on 8th July 1869, his fortieth birthday. "Thought much time wasted, & little done, made resolutions & determined to try to serve God more but I am sadly weak & irresolute." He probably felt that he was making insufficient progress with the rougher element of his parish, among whom he wanted to see less drunkenness, fewer illegitimate children and more piety. He may, on the other hand, have been feeling lonely and introspective. If so, the gap in his life would be filled only a few years later, on 17th January 1875, when he married Nellie Breach, a young woman more than twenty years his junior. They were married at Wallington, near Croydon, and then honeymooned in Bath, Exeter, Torquay, Babbacombe, Brixham and Bournemouth before returning to Burwash. Nellie proved very supportive and shared his interest in music. On their third wedding anniversary he observed that they had enjoyed "absolutely unclouded happiness." Over the years they had five children.

The Rev. Egerton is, of course, mainly remembered for his book *Sussex Folk and Sussex Ways*, which has the ponderous sub-title 'Stray Studies in the Wealden Formation of Human Nature'. The opening lines tell us much about the man and his sense of humour is immediately apparent.

"Though I have lived nearly the whole of my life in the country, country human nature is almost my only country taste. I am ashamed to own that I know hardly anything about the lives and habits of the birds, beasts and fishes which are to be found in my parish. Trees, ferns, and wild flowers afford me a real but sadly unscientific enjoyment; and with the geological formation of the district I have but a very superficial acquaintance, derived mainly from the various kinds of mud which I encounter in my parochial walks. With country people, however, I have a keen sympathy. Their habits of thought, their opinions, their prejudices, their superstitions, their manner of speech, their quaint expressions, their dry humour, their shrewd sense, their civilities, and even their harmless rudeness, have an interest for me which makes my country life a very happy one."

He goes on to tell us that the region is undergoing rapid change and that the manners and customs of the local people, with which he has long been familiar, will soon be extinct.

"I well know that the change must come but I own that I look forward with little satisfaction to the time when our boys and girls will all speak a uniform language prescribed by the Committee of Council on Education, and when our men and women will think only just as other people think."

Here we see his motive for recording the anecdotes and examples of rustic wisdom that were published as *Sussex Folk and Sussex Ways*. It was first printed serially in *The Leisure Hour* during 1881 and he was paid £20. It was then reprinted in *The Sussex Advertiser* during 1883 before being published as a book in 1884, when it was sold in paper covers for a shilling or cloth bound for two shillings.

The reviews were varied, *Notes and Queries* (28th June) reported that his book was 'full of genuine humour' but the *Pall Mall Gazette* (21st July) thought that Egerton's best stories illustrated the stupidity rather than wit of the rustics. The *Morning Post* (29th August) was also negative finding that the humour was often 'extremely difficult to discover.'

Humour is certainly apparent in the following anecdote, which concerns an encounter that Egerton had with a small boy who was completely unaware of the amusement his answers were affording. Egerton saw the boy in the village and as he did not recognise him asked whose little man he was.

    (He) "Father's."
    (Egerton) "Quite right; but where do you live?"
    (He) "Along wi' father."
    (Egerton) Yes, yes but where does your father live?"
    (He) "Why, he's our father - he lives along wi' us."
    At this point Egerton gave up and retired discomfited!

Egerton's main pastime was music, which he regarded as the one pure art, and his book includes an anecdote concerning a village concert at which he was the conductor. After some fifty voices had sung the Hallelujah Chorus with great gusto the audience demanded an encore and it was duly given. Then, at the end, when he thought that the greatness of the music should have been in all their minds, he saw one of his singers mop his perspiring brow and mutter "Well, that's a sweater!"

By 1885 Queen Victoria had heard of his book and made it known via her private secretary, Sir Henry Ponsonby, that she would be pleased to accept a copy. Egerton promptly had one specially bound and despatched but we do not know whether she liked it or whether, like the *Morning Post*'s reviewer, she was not amused!

After a month's illness Egerton died from heart failure in March 1888. There can be no doubt that he was sorely missed because several of his parishioners begged to be allowed to see him in his coffin and his friend, Henry Wace, recorded that "he almost lay in state like an emperor." After his burial a local committee launched a subscription to fund a memorial. They had it in mind to install a clock in the tower, but the fund exceeded their expectations and they found that could also afford to carry out much needed repairs and replace the churchyard gates.

Sussex Folk and Sussex Ways remained popular and a new edition was published by Chatto & Windus in 1892, with additional material including an obituary notice (reprinted from the *Guardian* of 18th April 1888) and the text of a lecture that Egerton had given on the history of Burwash. A third edition, published by Methuen, followed in 1924, with a sixteen-page preface by the Sussex novelist, Sheila Kaye-Smith.

EDWARD BOYS ELLMAN

Recollections of a Sussex Parson, 1912.

The Reverend Edward Boys Ellman's memoir, *Recollections of a Sussex Parson*, was published a few years after his death and nearly a century after his birth. He began to record his recollections in 1889 and wondered if any other period of history had known such great changes as he had witnessed in his lifetime. His memory was undimmed and he often describes fascinating details of life at the beginning of the nineteenth century, the sort of minutiae that are usually ignored in more conventional histories and biographies. The memoir is also highly anecdotal and many of his anecdotes are amusing.

He was born at Firle, in 1815, three months after the Battle of Waterloo, the fourth child and third son of John Ellman and his wife, Catherine (Boys). His grandfather was John Ellman of Glynde, who so famously improved the indigenous Southdown breed of sheep. On his mother's side one uncle was a naval officer and another was a parson.

Soon after his birth the family moved to the Manor, Southover, so that the elder boys could go to Lewes Grammar School but his father continued farming at Beddingham and Rype and went to church at Beddingham on Sundays to make sure that his labourers were also attending.

Ellman believed that his father had thought him dull in comparison with his brother, Frederic, who was something of a favourite, and the

Rev. Edward Boys Ellman aged 88

eldest of the boys, Spencer, was categorised as incorrigibly mischievous. Ellman recalled one of Spencer's pranks. On an evening when their parents' dinner guests included a Royal Duke the boys were watching proceedings from the top of the stairs. Maids were bringing the food to a table outside the dining room and removing empty dishes while footmen served the guests. Spencer had an idea and collected some young rabbits he had recently been given. He then waited for an opportunity and when it came put them on a plate and placed a cover over them. A waiter emerged from the dining room, collected what appeared to be another dish, took it in and removed the cover with a flourish. The boys heard laughter from the guests but their father was very angry.

The presence of a Royal Duke was not extraordinary for both his father and grandfather entertained many of the great men of their time. Ellman recalled seeing the Duke of Wellington both before and after he was Prime Minister and George Canning before he reached that high office. The news of Canning forming a government was brought to them by one of their grooms who said "Please sir, Mr Saxby (the postmaster) says I am to tell you that Mr Canning is a very good minister." To him the word 'prime' had only one meaning, 'very good.'

Ellman went to the Grammar School in Lewes in 1822 when its headmaster was George Proctor. When Proctor moved to Queen Elizabeth's College, Guernsey, in 1829, Ellman was among the pupils that moved with him. In 1832 Proctor moved to Chichester House, Kemp Town, Brighton, where he established an academy for young gentlemen, and once again Ellman moved with him. The school attracted several aristocratic boys and Harrison Ainsworth asserted that it was the prototype for Dr Blimber's Academy in *Dombey and Son*. It certainly matched Dickens' description of a fine house fronting the sea. While Ellman was there he often saw King William IV being driven along the seafront and the king always acknowledged his bow.

In February 1834 Ellman went up to Wadham College, Oxford to take the entrance exam and performed so badly that he believed he would have failed if he had not been accompanied by an uncle who had been at Wadham and was a great friend of one of the tutors. While he was at Oxford he decided that he would take Holy Orders and after visiting his brother Spencer, who by this time had joined the navy, he thought that he would like to be a naval chaplain. His father had other ideas and purchased the advowson of Berwick, so that his son could succeed its ageing incumbent, the Rev. Harry West.

West was typical of many rural vicars in the area who chose to live in Lewes rather than their parishes. The town was commonly known as the 'Rookery' because so many parsons rode out in black coats each Sunday. West, however, didn't even bother to visit Berwick on Sundays, preferring to leave his tedious parochial duties to a Curate-in-charge. At the time he was living in Ellman's former home Southover manor, Ellman' father having moved to Glynde in 1832, and it was there that Ellman first met him. West said that he had had endless trouble with his curates and suggested that Ellman might like to replace the present one at the same salary, £40 per annum. Ellman agreed, was ordained in September and immediately took over the parish. He remained curate for the next six and a half years during which time West never visited the parish once or showed any interest whatsoever in its affairs. Without any pastoral training Ellman simply got on with the job. He was a young man who took his responsibilities seriously and he worked hard.

In 1844 Ellman was invited to become vicar of Wartling. The late vicar had been accidentally shot and the unfortunate man's father, who held the advowson, had not decided whether or not to sell it. Eventually, it was agreed that Ellman could have the living on the understanding that he would resign it as soon as West died and he was able to become Rector at Berwick.

West died two years later and Ellman moved to Berwick where he remained until he died, sixty years later. He was unable to move into the old Rectory for it was in a terrible state of repair. It was so bad that the 'dilapidations' were adjudged at £900 and he concluded that his best plan would be to pull it down and build a new house. He had hoped to get married when the house was ready but he told nobody and made no protest when his eldest sister and her children came to live with him. He just turned his mind to the welfare of the parish and began saving so that he would be able to build a village school.

In 1853 his sister moved on and without further hesitation he proposed to Georgina Plummer, a young woman he had long known, and they were married before the year was out. They were an undemonstrative couple who often spent whole evenings together

Berwick Rectory

without exchanging more than a few words, he writing or reading and she reading or doing needlework. They were, nonetheless, happy and their personalities complemented one another; where he was sometimes too gentle she could speak firmly and sharply. Both of them were content to lead quiet lives of self-denial, devoting their energies to the welfare of others.

Largely at his own expense a small village school was completed in 1854 and he then turned his attention to the church, which was in a ruinous state. The spire had been struck by lightning a hundred years earlier, and had burned down. The tower was damaged, the north aisle had been pulled down because it had become dangerous, the yard outside sloped almost up to the windows of the south aisle, the roof was a rabbit warren, and the floor was rotten. He put a proposal to his parishioners that he would pay for a new vestry, rebuilding the spire and restoring the chancel if they would voluntarily levy a rate on every villager for two years to cover the remaining expenditure. They agreed but did not raise enough to cover all the expense. He had to find further money and Georgina sold her jewels to buy a chalice and paten.

The restored church was reopened on 21st December 1856 and Ellman's daughter, Maude, was christened on that day.

Mark Anthony Lower thought that the church had been "carefully restored" and we cannot doubt that Ellman efforts were well intentioned but the verdict in the *Sussex* volume of the Penguin 'Buildings of England Series' is that the church "suffered much at the hands of the restorer of 1856." The north arcade that he rebuilt is described as illiterate and clumsy on top and the chancel arch that he inserted is similarly damned.

Church services were very simple when Ellman first went to Berwick but he gradually introduced innovations. In 1857 he had the church decorated with flowers for Easter; they were then introduced for other festivals and ultimately for every Sunday. Later he started chanting the Canticles and celebrated Holy Communion with increasing frequency. He had to move cautiously for the villagers were suspicious of anything that seemed 'Popish', but he would probably have liked to go further for he sympathised with the high-church ideals of the Oxford Movement.

Ellman was, in many ways, a model Victorian vicar. His faith was firm and he lived by it. He toured his parish tirelessly, visiting the sick and enquiring about anyone he had not seen at church or any child who had missed school. He taught at the school and, from 1861, ran evening classes at the Rectory.

In November 1884 he had a seizure but recovered and it was his wife Georgina who died first. He died on 22 February 1906.

ALFRED ARTHUR EVANS

On Foot in Sussex, 1933.

A Saunterer in Sussex, 1935.

By Weald and Down, 1939.

The bare essentials of the early career of Alfred Arthur Evans are soon told. He was born in Hampshire in 1862, completed his education at the University of Durham, and was then ordained. For the best part of twenty years he served as curate in a succession of parishes and it was his fourth appointment that brought him to Sussex, to the parish Framfield, in 1897. He then moved to Arundel in 1899, to Slinfold in 1901, to Clapham with Patcham in 1902 and to Pevensey in 1904 before being inducted to the living of Friston with East Dean in 1908. He remained there for the next 21 years and after he had retired wrote the following comments on his tenure.

"Thirty years ago I entered, as vicar, into a Downland parish of 4,000 acres and 400 people and, I should add, less than £200 a year to maintain myself, keep up a large parsonage, which was old and continually needing repair, and a garden of nearly two acres. It was the beginning of the happiest period of my life; also I am bound to add, of a penurious one. I had to eat the bread of carefulness."

The Rev. Edward Boys Ellman tells us that in his youth many of the rural vicars in East Sussex lived well and that some "used constantly to hunt." but those halcyon days were long gone when Parson Evans took up his duties. In chapter VIII of *A Saunterer in Sussex* he claimed that he had very little leisure.

"There are people who imagine a country parson's life is a

perpetual holiday. He has, these fanciful folk say, a charming old vicarage and a charming old garden and lives among peaceful rural surroundings. It sounds tranquil and caterpillar-like. But there is another side. I have had two churches to serve, two parishes united in order to make a 'living', with remote farmsteads and cottages to visit covering 4,000 acres. A country parson is, or he certainly should be, a general factotum, a maid-of-all-work; it is his duty to mind everybody's business and not neglect his own."

He undoubtedly took his duties seriously but he probably overstates the case to make his point. Over the years he found plenty of time for activities that were not directly concerned with his ministry. He was an active member of the Sussex Archaeological Society; was an elected member of the Eastbourne Rural District Council for 14 years; and was vice-president of both the Eastbourne Natural History Society and the Sussex Beekeepers Association. Latterly, he was also a regular contributor to *Sussex County Magazine*, *The Sussex County Herald*, the *Chichester Diocesan Gazette* and *Home Words*.

Whenever he could get away he invariably went rambling and a picture taken on holiday in 1908 shows a slim man in a dark suit with his trousers tucked into long socks. He is wearing a straw boater, has a number of books under his arm and is leaning against a large rusty anchor. J.E. Ray of Hastings, who accompanied him on that trip, took the photograph near the Ypres Tower in Rye after they had spent four days walking through villages on the border of Sussex and Kent. Other photographs of Evans taken by Ray at around that date include one of him outside Arlington church with the local vicar, two schoolmasters and a doctor, all fellow members of the Sussex Archaeological Society, and one taken in the garden at East Dean where Evans is captured on the lawn with his pet collie, 'Scott'. He used to take the dog with him when he visited the local school to give scripture lessons and Scott invariably sat on a desk at the front of the class until the head-teacher found out and objected!

One of the things that marked Evans out from many other parsons was his interest in gypsies. He gained their trust, some of them became enduring friends and several called on him to have their children baptised. His reputation was so well known that a letter one of them posted in London reached him although it was only addressed "to the passon wat lives at deen". His reputation also encouraged visits from tramps and vagabonds, some of whom were disreputable, but they were all received with equal courtesy. He gave them cocoa, bread and jam, and explains, in chapter XVI of *A Saunterer in Sussex*, that he received in return, several fascinating pieces of road-lore, glimpses of an underworld, and much amusement.

In July 1929, as he approached his 67th birthday, he decided to retire. His health was no longer good enough for him to continue his ministry in a rural parish but he hoped to "read more books and perhaps do more writing". He moved to a small house at 15 North Pallant, in the charming south-east quarter of Chichester and did indeed do more writing. He continued to write for the *Sussex County Magazine*, *The Sussex County Herald* and the *Chichester Diocesan Gazette* and produced three books.

Evans looked frail but he continued to take long walks, sometimes with friends like Tickner Edwardes at Burpham, and wrote about everything he saw and heard. In his discursive column, 'A Countryman's Diary', he described birds, insects, flowers, folklore, church architecture, gypsies and other people that he met on his walks. He was particularly sound on church architecture and the wild flowers of Sussex. The first of his books, *On Foot in Sussex*, which utilised material from his magazine and newspaper articles, came about through the encouragement of E.V. Lucas, then chairman of Methuen's and it was published in 1933. *A Saunterer in Sussex* followed in 1935 and *By Weald and Down* in 1939. Each book is packed with varied material that will never be found in travel guides for his objective was to write about unfamiliar facets of the county. In *On Foot in Sussex* he explained that most of his subject matter lay off the beaten track where it would never be seen by people who were "chary of using the means of locomotion God provided them with". Typical chapter headings include 'The Joys of

Loitering', 'Flowers of an Old Wall', 'Pagham Episcopi', 'By the River Adur', 'The Inns of Sussex', 'Medieval Graffiti' and 'Downland at Night'. He took pleasure in much that he discovered along remote country lanes in Sussex and successfully conveyed that pleasure to his readers.

He kept writing almost to the end of his life and the last 'Countryman's Diary' that he wrote was printed in the February 1946 issue of the *Sussex County Magazine*, just two months before he died.

THOMAS GEERING

Our Parish: A Medley, 1884.

Our Sussex Parish, 1925.

Arthur Beckett, who was something of an authority on Sussex literature, declared that *Our Parish* by Thomas Geering was his favourite Sussex book. He was browsing through second-hand books in a shop when he first came across it and he only had to peruse a few pages to realise that he had found a rare treasure. He was also puzzled, for it was a book that was completely unknown to him. The copy he had discovered was titled *Our Parish: A Medley* by T.G.H. and had been published in 1884. From the signature following the preface he saw that T.G. was Thomas Geering and he deduced that the 'H' referred to Hailsham. He made a point of finding out about Geering, who had died many years earlier, and had the good fortune to meet the author's daughter, Emma, who was still living in Hailsham.

Beckett devoted the best part of a chapter of his book, *The Wonderful Weald*, to Geering's work and his readers began to look for copies of *Our Parish*. Unfortunately, these were both rare and costly. Beckett then persuaded Methuen to republish the book and it appeared as *Our Sussex Parish* in 1925. It is, essentially, a collection of essays and the 1925 edition differs from that of 1884 in that Beckett grouped them under three headings, 'Our Sussex parish and its institutions', 'Some personalities in our parish' and 'Sketches and tales of our parish'. Beckett also excluded a few of the essays as he thought that the earlier book had been too long. More recently, in 2001, Piccadilly Rare Books of Ticehurst issued a limited edition of just 100 copies.

Thomas Geering was born in Hailsham in 1813 and lived his whole life in the town. His father, also Thomas Geering, came from Alfriston where he had begun his working life as a shepherd's boy and a ploughboy before becoming a shoemaker. In November 1812 he married Elizabeth Holman, the eldest daughter of a yeoman of Hellingly, in the

Ebenezer Chapel at Alfriston and in the following year they moved to Hailsham.

Young Thomas received his education in Hailsham at the 'Academy' of Thomas Weston and he tells us that it "was THE school of the place", despite Weston's self avowed fondness for sherry. When drinking he had been known to say, with a touch of humour, that he wished his neck could be as long as his arm!

When he left school Geering was apprenticed to a Hailsham currier and in due course took over his father's business. It had been prospering and when his parent's died he inherited a house and a shop in the High Street. The business continued to prosper under his management and he was able to build a workshop where he employed a number of men. He was, as he explains, one of the elite of the town, for they had no squire and tradesmen were the only aristocracy in Hailsham!

Thomas Geering was widely read and Arthur Beckett was convinced that the Essays of Lamb had influenced his style. His favourite leisure activity seems to have been going out with his dog and gun but he also a good flute player.

It was only in 1879, when Geering was well into his sixties, that the idea of being an author dawned on him. He had just become acquainted with a writer who had moved into the area and was allowed to read some of his manuscripts. Geering began to ask himself why he should not also write, but he was hesitant. He wondered what he could write about because he had had no adventures; he had never even lived outside the parish. Happily, he overcame these inhibitions and proved that he had a natural ability. Most of the pieces that make up *Our Parish* first appeared in the columns of a country newspaper. They were then collected under the title *Our Parish: A Medley* and five hundred copies were published in 1884. These were sold under paper covers at eighteen pence or with a cloth binding for half-a-crown. Sales were slow and it was not a financial success. It was only a quarter of a century later, when Arthur Beckett drew it to the attention of a wider public, that its merits were eventually recognised.

THOMAS HORSFIELD

The History and Antiquities of Lewes and its Vicinity, 1827-35.

History, Antiquities and Topography of the County of Sussex, 1835

The story of how Thomas Horsfield came to write his monumental work, *History, Antiquities and Topography of the County of Sussex*, begins in the eighteenth century when a number of professional gentlemen with antiquarian inclinations collected much of the material that he utilised. The most significant of them was Sir William Burrell (1732-1796) an eminent lawyer, politician and commissioner of Excise who, despite a busy professional life, found the time to assemble a vast collection of documents and pictures for a projected 'History of Sussex.' Between 1771 and 1791 he took notes from published sources, transcribed manuscript material and, undertook several summer tours of Sussex copying monumental inscriptions and recording extracts from parish registers. He also commissioned three artists, James Lambert, Lambert's nephew of the same name, and Samuel Grimm, to travel the length and breadth of the county drawing and painting churches, notable houses and other antiquities. Ill health prevented Burrell from completing his project but he bequeathed his collection, which comprised fifteen folio volumes of manuscript notes and eight large volumes of drawings to the British Museum and they have proved invaluable to successive generations of historians.

One of the men who made early use of the Burrell material was Frederick Shoberl (1775-1853). His fairly comprehensive coverage of Sussex first appeared in 1813 as part of *The Beauties of England and Wales* and then separately as *A Topographical and Historical Description of the County of Sussex*. The latter has an interesting list of the principal books, maps and views of Sussex that had already been published and Shoberl informs us that other histories were being prepared when he went to press.

Working under the patronage of the 11th Duke of Norfolk the Rev.

James Dallaway (1763-1834) was preparing *A History of the Western Division of the County of Sussex* and John Fuller of Rose Hill in Brightling (1757-1834) was interesting himself in a similar work devoted to the eastern Rapes. As it turned out, the first project encountered problems and the second came to nothing. The first volume of Dallaway's History, which comprised preliminary observations and coverage of the City and Rape of Chichester, was published in 1815 and attracted criticism for the number of careless mistakes it contained. Perhaps as a consequence of this shortcoming, or because the price was too high, only 125 of the 500 copies that had been printed were sold by June 1819 when the rest were destroyed in a fire at the premises of the printer. To make matters worse the first part of a second volume, dealing with the Rape of Arundel, had only just been printed and the fire destroyed all but 60 copies that had been sent out for stitching. In 1822 Dallaway, stood down and the Rev. Edmund Cartwright (1773-1833) took over. He dealt with the Rape of Bramber in a volume that came out in 1830 and, after making some corrections and additions to the Arundel volume had 200 copies of it printed in 1832. He also began to work on a further book about the three western Rapes but died early in the following year.

It was at this point that an enterprising Lewes printer, John Baxter, saw an opportunity. He purchased Cartwright's incomplete manuscript and all the remaining Dallaway and Cartwright volumes, along with the copyright, plates and wood engravings and then commissioned Thomas Horsfield to prepare the first truly comprehensive county history.

Pastor Horsfield was a zealous nonconformist minister who had already written a successful work, *The History and Antiquities of Lewes and its Vicinity*. It had been published by Baxter in two volumes and on the strength of the first, which appeared in 1824, Horsfield had been elected a Fellow of the Society of Antiquaries. The second volume had followed in 1827.

Encouraged by the success of that work Horsfield had contemplated writing a 'History of Brighton and the Sussex Coast' and had advertised for material in the *Brighton Herald*, but he was pre-empted by J.D. Parry, whose *Historical and Descriptive Account of the Coast of Sussex* was published in 1833. Fortunately, his disappointment coincided with Baxter's acquisition of the Dallaway and Cartwright material and

Horsfield accepted Baxter's invitation to produce a county history for publication in two volumes. Horsfield was no longer living in Lewes but the quantity of material that was already available must have given him the confidence to do the work remotely.

Thomas Walker Horsfield was a Yorkshireman, born at Sheffield in 1792, who, after completing his studies at the Unitarian Academy in Hackney, had accepted an invitation to become minister at the Westgate Chapel in Lewes. When accepting the offer at the beginning of 1817 he made it clear that he did not find the smallness of their congregation or the slender income on offer at all encouraging. He also made his acceptance conditional on him being permitted to introduce doctrinal preaching and take a three-week holiday. In a separate letter, addressed only to the chairman of the congregation, he intimated that he wanted to do away with Watt's *Psalms and Hymns* in favour of a hymnal with a wider range of authorship. He also asked if they had any plans to make the chapel more comfortable as he found its appearance forbidding! Horsfield did not mince his words.

He was initially engaged for just one year but well before it had expired he was invited to continue in the post indefinitely. He had begun his ministry with great zeal and his doctrinal lectures had attracted crowds, especially, we are told, "from the class of inquiring young men." In June 1818 he was married to Hannah Waterhouse and it was doubtless with the object of increasing his income that he established and ran a successful school on St Anne's Hill. He then took a leading part in the foundation of a Mechanic's Institute and lectured there on chemistry, electricity and galvanism. That he also found time to write a history of Lewes is a tribute to his industry.

Horsfield's political views were fiercely liberal and came to prominence during the election of 1826 when he seconded the nomination of a radical candidate, Alexander Donovan, in opposition to two establishment figures, Sir John Shelley (Tory) and Thomas Reade Kemp (Whig). The most controversial issue at that election was Catholic Emancipation and Horsfield was noisome in his support. As a Unitarian, he believed fervently in freedom of worship but a great many of the town's Dissenters and Anglicans were immovably anti-Catholic. Feelings ran high and he made enemies. Donovan was defeated but Horsfield had stirred up a hornet's nest and he soon began to suffer the consequences. Parents were asked if they thought that such a dangerous radical was a fit person to teach their children and pupils were withdrawn from his school. With a large family to support he could not ignore the fall in his income and was left with no alternative but to seek an appointment with a higher stipend. In December 1827 became minister at the Mary Street Chapel in Taunton, Somerset.

It was in Taunton that Horsfield produced his *History of Sussex* and we can only speculate as to how much original work he had to undertake. The bulk of his task may have boiled down to editing for he had Cartwright's last manuscript, which may not have needed much alteration, as well as material that had been compiled by William Durrant Cooper on several of the eastern parishes. To supplement this Baxter solicited contributions on specialist topics such as geology, agriculture, climate, botany and parliamentary history from local specialists. He also took care to ensure that Horsfield's text for each parish was checked by a third party familiar with the place. He did not want the new *History* to incur the sort of criticisms that had bedevilled the work of Dallaway.

As the work approached completion Baxter set the price at a level that would put it within the reach of a much wider market than was usual and attracted over a thousand subscribers before going to press. *The History, Antiquities and Topography of the County of Sussex*, was at last published in 1835, in two large quarto volumes, lavishly illustrated and bound in quarter roan. They are impressive tomes and Horsfield must have been pleased with his magnum opus even if he does not deserve full credit for its authorship.

In the same year that his *History of Sussex* was published Horsfield moved to Chowbent Chapel at Atherton in Lancashire, and died there two years afterwards, aged only 45. His widow, Hannah, received "a special mark of kind benevolence" from Queen Victoria, and this must have been very welcome because she had seven children to support.

W.H. HUDSON
Nature in Downland, 1900.

W.H. Hudson did not visit Sussex until he was in his forties but he came to know the hills above Shoreham and Worthing as well as the back of his hand and wrote one of the best books about the South Downs, *Nature in Downland*.

William Henry Hudson was born in Argentina in 1841, at Quilmes, and was baptised at the English Methodist Church in nearby Buenos Aires. On his father's side his ancestry was Devonian, while his mother, who came from Maine, was descended from one of the 'Pilgrim Fathers'. He grew up in the countryside of the Rio de la Plata and from the age of six was allowed to ride his pony wherever he pleased. He wrote that he ran wild in a wild land and it gave him a passion for the natural world that he never lost. Then, in his fifteenth year, he suffered a severe attack of typhus and before he had fully recovered caught rheumatic fever. It left his heart weakened and he was told that he should do no active work. As a consequence he became increasingly studious and introspective.

From 1869 he was regularly in touch with Dr Sclater, secretary to the London Zoological Society, and sent him a number of short articles, which were published in the *Proceedings* of the society. These were his first literary efforts and their publication may have encouraged him to come to England.

When he sailed for England in 1874, aboard the steamship, *Ebro*, he was looking forward to seeing the countryside of his ancestral homeland; but he was destined to spend most of the rest of his life in London. For some years he lived in comparative poverty and little is known about this period except that he married his landlady, Emily Wingrave, in 1876. She was a former opera singer nearly fifteen years his senior who was then running a boarding-house at 11 Leinster Square, Bayswater. Their relationship did not turn out to be a love match but they gained companionship and while he wrote she sought to make a living from paying guests. While they were in Bayswater Hudson had the good fortune to meet a young writer, Morley Roberts, who became one of his closest friends. Roberts went to 11 Leinster Square to see someone who was boarding there and Hudson opened the front door. Roberts was immediately impressed by the tall gaunt figure facing him, judging that he was at once both kindly and formidable.

The boarding house was a failure and in 1884 they moved to another in Southwick Crescent. It too failed to make money and for a time they went into lodgings in Ravenscourt Park. It was an awful period when they practically starved; living through one week on only a tin of cocoa and milk. Emily gave singing lessons and Hudson continued to write but nearly all of his manuscripts were rejected. Then, their life together having reached its nadir, Emily inherited Tower House, 40 St Luke's Road, Westbourne Park. The house was mortgaged almost to its full value but by living on the top floor and letting the lower ones they found that they could make ends meet. It was a strange fate for this enigmatic man who so loved being out of doors.

It was in 1888 that Hudson discovered Sussex and it came about through his friendship with Morley Roberts. After a trip overseas Roberts had settled in Chelsea amongst a colony of artists. Hudson came to know several of them including Thomas McCormick and Alfred Hartley who illustrated some of his later books. Hartley, encouraged Hudson and Roberts to join him on trips to Shoreham, where he liked to paint, and they went, often for short stays but sometimes for longer holidays. Morley recalled its appeal in his biography of Hudson.

"Shoreham in those still days, before its shingle beach was made an affront to nature and the sea by a ghastly agglomeration of hideous bungalows, greatly appealed to Hudson. The sea he always greeted by walking into the edge of the surf, there scooping up a handful of water, which he drank as some kind of ceremony which re-united him to the salt wildness of nature. But not only the sea was peculiarly grateful to him. He loved the whispering wide mud flats of the Adur, with their sandpipers at ebb tide, and that river's broad surface when the flood made and turned it into a great river which he rejoiced to see from the Downs above. They were his Downs, as one might say, at the back of the town: in those days made picturesque by an old windmill which afterwards perished by fire."

Hudson loved the downland and when he decided to make it the subject of a book he began to think about the essays that Richard Jefferies had written. He was convinced that if Jefferies had lived a little longer he would have written a book about the South Downs and the maritime district of Sussex, as good as anything he had ever done. With this in mind he arranged to stay at the cottage in Goring where Jefferies had died. He arrived in Goring on a gloomy September day in 1899 and as he walked down a narrow lane in search of the cottage it crossed his mind that Jefferies must often have passed that way. The crunch of gravel ahead of him caused him to look up and he believed that Jefferies was standing before him in the guise of a tramp. The man had a large nose and a long beard and his expression suggested anguish that was near to despair. After a moment the tramp asked if Hudson could spare a penny and the spell was broken. Hudson gave him something and passed on haunted by the memory of the man's eyes.

The book he began at Jefferies house in Goring was *Nature in Downland*, which proved to be an inspired piece of descriptive writing, liberally laced with anecdotes. Morley Roberts aptly described it as "Hudson's earliest masterpiece of simple and characteristic observation in England" and the following passage is a typical example of his descriptive prose.

> "The turf is composed of small grasses and clovers mixed with a great variety of creeping herbs, some exceedingly small. In a space of one square foot of ground, a dozen or twenty or more species of plants may be counted, and on turning up a piece of turf the innumerable interwoven roots have the appearance of cocoa-nut matting. It is this thick layer of interlaced fibres that gives the turf its springiness, and makes it so delightful to walk upon."

The book is comprehensive in its coverage of the landscape, its people, flowers, animals, insects and birds and it has a strong sense of coherence. It has been described as having an almost symphonic pattern; the opening chapter, with Hudson sitting on the crest of Kingston Hill, having the suggestive complexity of the first movement of a symphony and the succeeding chapters being developments of the themes that it contains.

The penultimate chapter provides an element of dramatic contrast when Hudson deals with Chichester for he did not like the city. "Chichester" he wrote, "is not in itself sacred, nor pleasant, nor fragrant to the nostrils." A diatribe follows in which he writes about its largely empty churches and its seventy odd public houses where "the perpetual swilling" turned his stomach. As always, Hudson's prose is direct and descriptive.

W.H. Hudson
after a portrait by Frank Brooks

Despite the quality of his prose, Hudson was earning very little from book sales and an influential friend approached the government to see if he could be given a civil list pension. It was agreed and in 1901 he was awarded £150 a year in recognition of the originality of his writing on Natural History. In modern political jargon it was probably 'too little and too late' but it was very welcome. He said that it made him a rich man and it certainly gave him the freedom to spend more of his time out of London.

By 1914 his wife was unwell and he took her to Worthing in the hope that it might improve her health. The location seemed to suit her and they concluded that she should move there leaving him in London. Emily settled initially at a boarding house a few minutes from the sea, a rambling property that has since been demolished. After three years she moved to another boarding house in the Steyne, later still to one at 8 Bedford Row and finally to 3 Woodleigh Road, West Tarring, where she died in 1921. Hudson visited her regularly throughout this period but did not acquire a good opinion of Worthing. He told Morley Roberts that he hated the place. "It is all talk, talk, talk, but never a gleam of an original or fresh remark or view of anything that does not come out of a book or newspaper."

He died little over a year after his wife and was buried alongside her in Broadwater Cemetery. He had wanted a burial plot close to the grave of Richard Jefferies but could not get one and their graves are to be found in another part of the cemetery.

Richard Jefferies

Nature near London, 1883.

The Life of the Fields, 1884.

The Open Air, 1885.

Field and Hedgerow, 1889.

Richard Jefferies was born in Wiltshire and grew up there but much of his finest writing was done after he moved to Sussex in 1881. He was born on 6th November 1848, at Coate Farm in the north Wiltshire parish of Chisledon and lived there until he got married in 1874. As a boy he enjoyed the usual pursuits of country children of that period, climbing trees, fishing and shooting; but he also enjoyed being alone and was already acutely sensitive to the beauty of the natural world around him. He also spent time in Sydenham with his aunt and uncle, the Harrilds, and went on holidays to Sussex with them. They were happy episodes and when he was nineteen he wrote to his aunt declaring "I always feel dull when I leave you. I am happier with you than at home." After leaving school he spent much of his time alone rambling and reading; and the only money that he earned came from the sale of any hares that he could snare or shoot. His family thought that he was indolent and one local wit observed that he was cut out to be a gentleman but lacked the money!

He joined the staff of the *North Wilts Herald* when he was seventeen and undertook a variety of duties including reporting and correcting manuscripts. After a serious illness in 1867 he moved to the *Wilts and Gloucestershire Standard* as a reporter and held the post for two years. It is not clear why he then left the *Standard* for he remained on good terms with his former boss and was re-employed in February 1872. Up to this time his writing was mundane. Then, in November 1872, he wrote an extraordinarily long and forceful letter to *The Times* about the parlous condition of agricultural labourers in Wiltshire. It brought him to the attention of the public and before long his work was being accepted by the *Pall Mall Gazette* and other national journals.

In July1874 he married an attractive young woman from a neighbouring farm, Jessie Baden, and after a few months they moved to Victoria Street, Swindon, where their first child was born. His first novel, *The Scarlet Shawl*, had just been published and by the end of that year he had completed another, *Restless Human Hearts*, which appeared in 1875. He seems to have hoped that fiction might add significantly to his earnings but neither novel stirred any public interest. It was only in short pieces about countryside matters that his true abilities were becoming apparent.

In 1877 the family moved to Surbiton, where they remained for five years, and it was in this suburban environment that he wrote his first country books. *The Gamekeeper at Home* appeared in 1878, *The Amateur Poacher* and *Wild Life in a Southern County* in 1879 and *Round about a Great Estate* in 1880. They were better than anything that he had previously written. He had discovered his true vocation and gained a reputation as a successor to Gilbert White of Selborne.

Then, in December 1881, he fell ill and had to undergo four operations during the following year. For the sake of his health they decided to move to the coast and settled at 'Savernake House', Lorna Road in a part of Hove that was then known as West Brighton. Jefferies already knew something of Sussex from holidays spent at Worthing and elsewhere when he was a boy and at Hastings when he was twenty-two. Now, as he recovered from surgery, he became more closely familiar with Brighton and its environs. His son, Harold, later recalled how much his father had loved the seafront where, when the weather was rough, they spent hours in the shelters watching the surf on the beach. There were also family visits to the two piers and the Aquarium, the latter being particularly popular if their arrival coincided with feeding time for the seals. Jefferies was weak but he was able to take some long solitary walks over the neighbouring downland and he continued to write.

While he was at Lorna Road his prose took on a heightened intensity and he wrote a remarkable autobiographical work, *The Story of My Heart*, in which he sought to explain the mystic consciousness that drove him. It contains no conventional account of his life but it makes strangely compulsive reading. He also wrote the last two essays in the collection entitled *Nature Near London*, all those in *The Life of the Fields* and some of those in *The Open Air*. It was a richly creative and productive period of his life.

The essays concerned wholly with Sussex are 'To Brighton', 'The Southdown Shepherd', and 'The Breeze on Beachy Head' in *Nature Near London*, 'Clematis Lane', 'Nature near Brighton', 'Sea, Sky and Down' and 'January in the Sussex Woods' in *The Life of the Fields*, and 'Sunny Brighton' and 'The Bathing Season' in *The Open Air*.

In the following passage from 'To Brighton' he describes the illusory appearance of the South Downs and the point that he makes will be familiar to everyone who loves walking on them.

"So easy is the outline of the ridge, so broad and flowing are the slopes, that those who have not mounted them cannot grasp the idea of their real height and steepness. The copse upon the summit yonder looks but a short stroll distant; how much you would be deceived did you attempt to walk thither! The ascent here in front seems nothing, but you must rest before you have reached a third of the way up. Ditchling Beacon there, on the left, is the very highest above the sea of the whole mighty range, but so great is the mass of the hill that the glance does not realize it."

In 'Sunny Brighton' Jefferies showed that he did not only have eyes for the countryside. He gives a vivid description of the local fishermen and shows that he had an eye for the girls. "There are more handsome women in Brighton" he wrote, "than anywhere else in the world. They are so common that gradually the standard of taste in the mind rises and good-looking women who would be admired in other places pass by without notice."

In 1884 the family moved to Victoria Road, Eltham. He was still weak and his wife's selfless devotion should not be underestimated for, as one of their visitors observed, Jefferies was a man of moods and, like many invalids, his temper was uncertain. While they were at Eltham their youngest child died and Jefferies was so stricken with grief that he could not attend the funeral. By June of the following year they were back in Sussex and lodged at 'Rehoboth Villa', Jarvis Brook, Rotherfield until September when they moved to a small stone house in a bleak and windy position at Crowborough. It was called 'The Downs', and commanded fine views in every direction. For a time his strength improved and he was able to enjoy walking but he suffered a relapse and became weaker than ever. It was in this house that he wrote with his own hand for the last time; his subsequent essays being dictated to his wife. The essay he penned there, so painfully, was 'Hours of Spring', one of those included in *Field and Hedgerow*, which also included such locally inspired pieces as 'The Countryside, Sussex' and 'Buckhurst Park'.

By this time the tubercular condition of his lungs was chronic and a few of his friends raised funds privately to enable him to move to the coast where they hoped that he would find the sea air more congenial. By the end of 1886 the family had settled within 300 yards of the Channel at 'Sea View', Goring-by-Sea, but Jefferies was very weak, pale and skeletal. He could only walk short distances and almost everything he did caused him pain. When the weather was fine he spent time in the garden dictating to Jessie, but before long he became too weak to leave his bedroom.

He died on 14th August 1887 aged only 38 and was buried in Broadwater cemetery where a marble cross marks his grave. The inscription around the base reads "To the honoured memory of the Prose poet of England's Fields and Woodlands".

MARK ANTHONY LOWER

Contributions to Literature, 1854.

The Worthies of Sussex, 1865

A Compendious History of Sussex, 1870.

Mark Anthony Lower was the author of numerous works including *The Worthies of Sussex* and *A Compendious History of Sussex*; but he has another claim to fame as one of the founders of the Sussex Archaeological Society.

He was born in the village of Chiddingly in 1813, and was the youngest son of Richard Lower, village schoolmaster, land surveyor, general factotum and dialect poet. At the age of seventeen he followed his father into the teaching profession by assisting his sister at a school she had started in East Hoathly. Shortly afterwards he opened his own school at Cade Street, Heathfield, lodging there during the week and returning home at the weekends. He already had literary ambitions and his first book, *Sussex: Being a Historical, Topographical, and General Description of every Rape, Hundred, River, Town, Borough, Parish, Village, Hamlet, Castle, Monastery and Gentleman's Seat in that County*, was published in 1831. It was a substantial achievement for a teenager, but it did not live up to its ambitious title and he later regretted that it had been written.

After eighteen months at Heathfield he moved to Alfriston where he opened a larger school and while he was there used his spare time to learn Latin. At the same time he met John Dudeney, a self-educated shepherd who became one of his lifelong friends, and they jointly formed a so-called 'Mechanic's Institute' with the objective of encouraging reading and scientific pursuits. While walking between Alfriston and his home in Chiddingly, he used to call on farming friends in the parish of Ripe and there met and courted a flaxen-haired governess, Mercy Holman.

In 1835 he concluded that he had gained enough experience from his village school ventures and went to Lewes where he rented an old chapel or meeting house in Lancaster Street and established a school for middle-class boys. It prospered and in January 1838 he married Mercy Holman. There were further moves as his school and family grew and it was during this period that he issued a manifesto opposing the town's famous November 5th celebrations, which he described as a "Saturnalia of the Roughs." He put it out anonymously but his authorship became known and it made him very unpopular in some quarters.

In October 1845 a messenger called on Lower and asked him to hurry down to the ruins of the former Clunaic Priory where workmen who were making a cutting for the railway from Brighton had made a discovery. A workman's shovel had struck what he thought was a slab of stone but on closer inspection it proved to be a leaden box and a gentleman who had been watching the work immediately sent for the best known antiquaries in the town Mark Anthony Lower and William Figg. Two boxes were unearthed and the stunned observers saw that they bore the names 'Willelm' and 'Gundrada'. They had come upon the mortal remains of the once mighty Norman lord, William de Warrene, and his wife Gundrada, the lord and lady who had jointly founded the priory some 770 years earlier.

The discoveries were reported in *The Illustrated London News*, arousing national interest, and Lower wrote an account of the find for the British Archaeological Association.

The fever of interest that prevailed locally also stimulated Lower to write to William Blaauw, author of The *Baron's War*, with a proposal for the formation of a Sussex Archaeological Society. It was something they had discussed previously and the time now seemed ripe for action. A proposal was printed in both the *Sussex Advertiser* and the *Sussex Express* during May and an inaugural meeting was arranged. It was held at the County Hall, Lewes, on June 18th and the Society formally came into being. Blaauw was appointed Hon.

Secretary and both Lower and Figg were elected to the Committee. From then on Lower committed a disproportionate amount of his time to the society serving on committees, addressing meetings and writing papers. Only one of the 26 volumes of the *Sussex Archaeological Collections* that were published during his lifetime lacked any contribution from him. His papers were, however, as L.F. Salzman, one of the most distinguished editors of the *Collections* has observed, "of very uneven merit."

Around 1853 Lower moved to St Anne's House, a large red-brick building, which has since been demolished, and remained there for more than a decade. His enthusiasm for matters concerning the Sussex Archaeological Society was now boundless; he began to neglect his school and pupil numbers fell.

When his wife, Mercy, died at the end of May 1867 he sold his house and moved to Seaford where he took just a few French pupils; preferring to devote most of his time to writing.

His literary output was already prodigious and included a number of works concerned wholly with Sussex. *Contributions to Literature* is a miscellany of articles and essays on topics like local nomenclature, the South Downs and the iron-works of south-east England. *The Worthies of Sussex* is a collection over two hundred biographical sketches of 'worthies' who were local or who made their names locally. It is a large tome that looks very handsome, half bound in the original red morocco. In 1870 he completed his *Compendious History of Sussex* which is organised by parish and includes useful cross-references to the first twenty volumes of the *Sussex Archaeological Collections*.

In 1870 he married Sarah Scrase, a lady he had known for a long time, and in 1871 they moved to the south London suburb of Peckham. He was no longer in the best of health and in 1873 they took a trip to Denmark and Sweden, hoping that it might prove beneficial. It did not and they had to return prematurely. Sarah died in 1875 and Lower's health having further declined he went to stay with his youngest daughter at Enfield, Middlesex, where he died in March 1876. He is buried in St Anne's, churchyard Lewes.

RICHARD LOWER
Stray Leaves from an Old Tree, 1862.

Richard Lower was born in Alfriston in 1782, the son of John Lower who owned and operated a barge, the *Good Intent,* on the river Cuckmere. Dickie Lower proved too frail to follow his father's trade but the Alfriston schoolmaster, Thomas Susan, was a good teacher and Dickie acquired sufficient learning to set up his own school at Muddles Green in the village of Chiddingly, in 1803. In the same year he married Mary (Polly) Oxley at Berwick.

Lower soon became a leading figure in Chiddingly, for it had no resident squire or clergyman and he became the general factotum. "He was," according to his son Mark Anthony Lower, "an excellent practical mathematician, and a land-surveyor of considerable note. He also held nearly every parochial office, made wills and agreements and was an acknowledged authority on every local matter."

When the Rev. A.A. Evans, who was vicar of East Dean and Friston from 1908 to 1929, visited Chiddingly he met villagers who could remember 'old Dickie Lower'. They recalled being 'whacked' by him when they were his pupils and said he had shown great faith in the birch rod. He also learned that Dickie has been a rather irascible man and concluded that he had probably been more feared than loved.

One of Lower's specialities was verse and he chronicled local events in rhyme for newspapers like the

Cover of an edition in paper wrappers

Sussex Advertiser. He is, however, best remembered as a dialect poet, his reputation resting on two long poems. The full title of the first was, *Tom Cladpole's Jurney to Lunnon, shewing the many difficulties he met with, and how he got home at last; told by himself, and written in pure Sussex doggerel, by his Uncle Tim*. In 1830 he had 18,000 copies printed in paper wrappers at his own expense and they sold rapidly. Its popularity was so great that thousands of 'pirate' copies were also printed, much to Lower's annoyance.

One of the great virtues of *Tom Cladpole's Jurney to Lunnon* is that the author had grown up with the dialect. He had heard it all his life and understood the thinking of the people who spoke it. Elements of the story are exaggerated for the sake of humour or pathos but the story struck a chord with Sussex villagers; they saw it as their literature and took it to their hearts.

Lower's second dialect poem came out in 1844 with the title *Jan Cladpole's Trip to Merricur giving an account of the white, black, and yellor folks wot he met wud in his travels in search arter dollar trees: and how he got rich enough to beg his way home: writ all in rhyme by his father, Tim Cladpole*. It is less spontaneous than the earlier work but was also popular.

Richard Lower's first and only book came out in 1862 with the title *Stray Leaves from an Old Tree: Selections from the Scribblings of an Octogenarian*. His son Mark Anthony Lower, who had by then become the proprietor of a successful school and a prominent antiquarian, helped him to put the selection together. It includes both *Tom Cladpole's Jurney to Lunnon* and *Jan Cladpole's Trip to Merricur*, revised and accompanied by a brief glossary. Most of the other 'stray leaves' are poems but none of them are in dialect and they are of indifferent merit. Fortunately, they are not entirely devoid of interest. One, which is entitled 'The Man of Business and Parish Fac-totum', undoubtedly describes Lower's own role in Chiddingly although he gives the factotum the name of 'Walter Wilkins'. Another lists the reasons why Lower gave up smoking a pipe when his children were young, but it seems that his resolution did not extend into old age. He confesses in a footnote that after forty years he is once again a smoker. After the two dialect poems the most interesting piece in the book is an essay in prose concerning 'Old Southdown Shepherds'. In it he recalls the days of 'tenantry flocks' when one shepherd looked after the sheep of many farmers and was paid by each according to the proportion of the flock that they owned.

Although Richard Lower wrote no more dialect verse his son, Mark Anthony translated the 'Song of Solomon' into dialect for Napoleon's nephew, Prince Lucien Buonaparte, who collected versions in several English dialects. Richard Lower mentions the prince in *Stray Leaves*, observing in dialect that the young man has copies of the Cladpole stories in "his libery at Lunnun", that he is "a gurt acquirer o' langwidges" and that his "ambition is a nobler one dan what de Empror's was."

In 1864 Lower began to feel his years and left Chiddingly to stay with one of his sons at Tonbridge in Kent. He died there on 29th September 1865 and we can only regret that during his busy life he did not find the time and inclination to write more dialect doggerel.

Such later dialect pieces as *Summat 'Bout Sussex an Sum Sussexers* which was privately printed in 1936, and *De Shepherd Psalm. Put in de Sussex Dialect* by Jim Cladpole, which followed in 1937, are by James Richards, formerly of Hailsham, who was living in Tunbridge Wells at the time.

E.V. LUCAS
Highways and Byways in Sussex, 1904.

When E.V. Lucas wrote to The Times in February 1938, on the subject of a threatened housing development on the South Downs at High Salvington, he described himself as "a loyal South Saxon". He was just that, despite the time that he spent in London, and his best-selling *Highways and Byways in Sussex* is still one of the best written and most comprehensive of the county guides.

Edward Verrall Lucas was born at Eltham, Kent, in 1868, the second of seven children of Alfred Lucas and his wife Jane (Drewitt). Both of his parents were Quakers from families with interests in farming, banking, shipping and brewing and his father would have succeeded to a partnership in a bank if he had not neglected his duties and been advised to seek another career. From then on Alfred Lucas never sought full-time employment and, in the words of his granddaughter, Audrey, "merely muddled about as an agent for various Insurance Companies and Building Societies." The family moved to Brighton soon after E.V. was born and he grew up in that town attending a succession of schools both locally and elsewhere. His father was a completely self-centred man who, for example, took his children to Brill's Baths, not in order that they might learn to swim but so that they could sit in the gallery and watch him enjoying himself! He also expected E.V. and his brother to bowl cricket balls to him before breakfast on summer mornings without ever giving either of them a chance to bat. More happily the family regularly watched cricket matches at the county ground in Hove and were enthusiastic fans of the great players of the day.

At the age of sixteen E.V. was apprenticed to a Brighton bookseller, Treacher, whose business occupied a bow-fronted building at the corner of North Street and East Street. Then at the age of 21 he joined the staff of the *Sussex Daily News* as a reporter. He might have remained with the paper indefinitely but, after two years, an Uncle, who was concerned about his career, gave him £200 to enable him to go to London and attend the lectures of W.P. Ker, Professor of English Literature at University College.

In April 1893, just as his funds ran out, E.V.L. was invited to join the *Globe*, a leading evening paper, and soon afterwards received his first commission for a book. It came from the official publisher of the Society of Friends who wanted a memoir of Bernard Barton, a Quaker poet who had been a friend of Charles Lamb.

Esther Meynell (then Moorhouse) remembered him at this time when he sometimes visited her parent's house in Patcham. She recalled that he was a quiet young man with a slow voice and a slow smile who was enthusiastic about English literature and could communicate that enthusiasm to others. She was still a schoolgirl but he took time to encourage her interest in literature and writing.

In 1897 he married Florence Griffin, the daughter of a colonel in the United States army, and they lived firstly in the Kentish Weald, in a cottage with the unprepossessing name of 'Froghole'. Their next home was in Kensington and their daughter, Audrey, recalled that while they were there Joseph Conrad and James Barrie were regular callers. In 1908 they returned to the countryside, to Kingston Manor, which lies at the foot of the Downs to the south-west of Lewes. While they were there E.V.L. liked to play the squire, presenting each cottage with an ornate canister of tea at Christmas, but the villagers never stopped seeing the Lucas family as 'people from London'. While they were at Kingston E.V.L. began to spend each Tuesday to Friday in London but the house was usually full at weekends and their visitors included such eminent literati as Arnold Bennett, John Galsworthy, A.E.W. Mason, Hugh Walpole and A.A. Milne.

By this time E.V.L. was a literary freelance but he gradually became more closely associated with Methuen's publishing company. It began when H.C. Beeching, who was editing Methuen's Little Library, asked him to write an introduction to the *Essays of Elia* and this in turn led to a commission from

E.V. Lucas circa 1930

Methuen himself, to produce a new edition of Lamb's works and a new biography. E.V.L. jumped at the opportunity for Lamb was his idol. *The Works of Charles and Mary Lamb* were issued in 7 volumes between 1903 and 1905 and his *Life of Charles Lamb* was published in two volumes in 1905. Methuen also began to employ E.V.L. as a Reader. At the same time he was contributing to *Punch*, and writing essays, novels and books on travel, art and topography.

From a Sussex viewpoint his most significant work was the Sussex volume he wrote for Macmillan's *Highways and Byways* series. It was very popular and remains one of the most interesting county guides. He described it as 'anecdotal topography' and it earned him a reputation as an authority on Sussex. The contents are not original, for he quotes liberally from earlier authors, but they are remarkably comprehensive and entertaining. Arthur Beckett hit the nail on the head when he described *Highways and Byways in Sussex* as "largely a compilation of what had already been written on Sussex, made more readable by the genius of one who was a journalist and master anthologist."

To take account of the changes that had affected Sussex since its publication in 1904 the book was updated, revised and reissued in 1936 and this second edition is to be preferred. In response to public demand Macmillan also issued the work in three pocket-sized volumes, titled 'West', 'Mid-' and 'East' Sussex.

E.V.L's interest in Sussex was real and he was an enthusiastic subscriber to Arthur Beckett's *Sussex County Magazine*, which was launched in December 1926. He wrote to the Rev. A.A. Evans congratulating him on the quality of his column, 'A Countryman's Diary', and it was he who persuaded Arthur Beckett to stop using the clumsy term 'Sussexian' in favour of the infinitely preferable 'South Saxon'. He also wrote some Sussex verse including a delightful untitled piece that describes how his thoughts would run if he were to be away from the county in springtime. The following is from an amusing piece he wrote for Lady Leconfield in 1918.

> We don't deny a certain share
> Of scenic merit here and there
> Beyond our borders. That's confessed.
> Sussex (we merely state) is best.

The family left Kingston Manor in 1912 and for a time returned to London, spending the summer and weekends at Coates Common near Fittleworth. Then in 1914 they moved to Tillington Cottage, Tillington, near Petworth, a property that E.V.L. renamed 'Dangerous Corner' because a prominent road sign with that warning stood close to the gate! Their stay at Tillington was disrupted by the war during which E.V.L. helped his wife to establish a home for refugee children in a French chateau at Bettancourt. He also spent time with the Red Cross in Italy.

After the war family life disintegrated and Audrey recalled that she only saw her father spasmodically for nearly a decade. He was working as hard as ever, especially for Methuen's and when Sir Algernon Methuen died in 1924 he was invited to succeed him as Chairman. Many exceptional Sussex books were published at this time and local writers like Hadrian Allcroft, A.A. Evans and Barclay Wills owed much to his encouragement.

At this time he had a small London flat and a country cottage in Sussex. The flat was simply a place where he slept and to which he returned to dress for dinner; for he spent his evenings with friends, mainly at restaurants or clubs. He had grown very autocratic and it was said that there was not a head waiter in London who did not respect his judgement and fear his tongue.

He went to the country cottage both at weekends and when he needed periods of quiet for sustained work.

Over the last decade of his life his contribution to literature, which amounted to nearly one hundred books, was recognised with honorary doctorates from Oxford and St Andrews and he was made a Companion of Honour in 1932. In his biography, *Reading, Writing and Remembering* he declared that if he ever retired and had the time he would 'granderize' Horsfield's *History of Sussex*. He never did find the time before dying in London on 26th June 1938.

GIDEON ALGERNON MANTELL

The Fossils of the South Downs, 1822.

Illustrations of the Geology of Sussex, 1827

A Day's Ramble in and about the Ancient Town of Lewes, 1846.

The Journal of Gideon Mantell, 1940 [ed., E. Cecil Curwen.]

Gideon Algernon Mantell (pronounced mantle) was a great pioneering geologist. He was the first person to demonstrate that freshwater had covered much of the Weald in Mesozoic times and from the fossils he found there he identified four out of the five genera of Dinosaurs that were known when he died, Iguanodon, Hylaeosaurus, Pelorosaurus and Regnosaurus.

He was born in 1790, in St Mary's Lane, Lewes, son of Thomas Mantell, a successful shoemaker, pious Methodist and a radical Whig. Gideon was sent firstly to a nearby dame school, then to John Button's Academy at Cliffe, and finally to a 'Dissenting Academy for Boys' in Wiltshire run by his Uncle George Mantell, a non-conformist minister. When he returned he was apprenticed to a Lewes surgeon, James Moore, for a term of five years and then spent six months at Bart's Hospital in London. Moore recognised his potential and took him into partnership as soon as he had qualified. Gideon made midwifery his speciality, attending between two and three hundred deliveries every year, and gained a high reputation locally. It was a good start for his career but he was fiercely ambitious and determined to achieve wider fame.

In 1816 he married Mary Ann Woodhouse at St Marylebone, London, and they made their home at 3 Castle Place, Lewes. The house was one of four that had been built on the High Street, just below the castle. Moore had purchased No.3 in 1815 and Mantell was renting it when he got married. Moore's health was already failing and in March 1818 Mantell bought out the partnership. A few months later he also bought the house and in the following year he bought the house next door so that they could be converted into one, which is now 166 High Street. The redesign included a new façade with giant pilasters surmounted by ammonite capitals and an elegant Ionic porch. It was impressive and made a very public statement about Mantell's ambitions.

Mantell was a tall, slim man with penetrating eyes, whose restless energy and insatiable curiosity were unbounded. He often rode twenty miles visiting forty or more patients in a day and whenever his time was not taken up with medical duties, he was out and about in pursuit of his other interests, geology and archaeology. He also found time to write poetry. Anyone who reads his journal will be struck by his exhausting lifestyle, which was only possible because he made a point of limiting himself to just four hours sleep each night.

He collected fossils both by his own efforts and by buying them from quarrymen. He also dug up several barrows in search of antiquities. No modern archaeologist could condone his poorly recorded treasure hunting but his pioneering geological researches were exemplary. He had been interested in fossils from boyhood and had begun by studying what could be found in the chalk hills around Lewes. His first geological article, 'On the Extraneous Fossils found in the Neighbourhood of Lewes', was printed in the *Sussex Weekly Advertiser* in 1812 and 'Of the strata in the vicinity of Lewes' followed in 1813. The latter resulted in his introduction to members of the Linnaen Society and in December 1813 he was elected a member. In the following year he wrote a paper on one of the fossils he had found near Lewes and it was read before the Society. It was also published in their *Transactions* and was the first of nearly fifty scientific papers he would write.

When his explorations took him further afield he was thrilled to find that the Wealden strata was exposed to a depth of 40 feet in a quarry at Whiteman's Green, near Cuckfield. The site became even more interesting when he saw that the fossils in the layers of sandstone and limestone were unlike any he had discovered in the chalk hills near Lewes. He paid one of the quarrymen to supply him with any that he found and the site became a very fruitful source. He soon realised that he was looking at specimens that were much older than those he had previously collected; he had puzzling evidence of tropical flora and fragments of some very large bones.

His first book, *The Fossils of the South Downs*, was published in May 1822 with illustrations drawn by his wife. In it he classified the strata of Sussex and gave the geological designation 'Tilgate Beds' to the fossil rich strata he had seen in the Whiteman's Green quarries, after the Tilgate Forest in which they were situated. Looking back with all the benefit of hindsight it is clear that the book has historic significance, both for having the first description of dinosaur remains correctly described as giant lizards and for his conclusion that the 'Tilgate Beds' were of freshwater origin. It was favourably reviewed but his expectations had been far too high and he ended the year with a sense of disappointment. He had hoped that it would open doors but it did not and he concluded that this was because he was known to be the son of a shoemaker. "In fact" he wrote, "I perceive so many chances against my surmounting the prejudice which the humble situation of my family naturally excites in the minds of the great that I have serious thoughts of trying my fortune either at Brighton or London."

For the time being he remained in Lewes performing his medical duties and pursuing his fossil collecting with undiminished energy. He was particularly interested in a number of fossilised teeth from the sandstone of Tilgate Forest and was convinced that they had belonged to a gigantic herbivorous reptile that had lived there in what we now know as the Cretaceous period. It was a startling theory for nothing like it had been postulated before and it was not accepted until he received the support of the leading French authority, Georges Cuvier. Mantell then established that the teeth resembled those of an iguana, although they were twenty times as large, and on this basis he named the creature Iguanadon. He had discovered a dinosaur but the term 'dinosaur' had not yet been coined. It has been suggested that his wife found the first of the teeth but there is no firm basis for the story.

At the beginning of 1825 a paper he had written on the Iguanodon was read before the Royal Society and neither the name he had coined nor his general conclusions were challenged. Then, in December, he received the accolade he had long coveted, he was elected a Fellow.

In 1826 he was temporarily distracted from geology by a completely different matter. He looked in at the local Assizes to see something of the trial of Hannah Russell who was accused of poisoning her husband and heard the evidence given by the surgeon who had carried out the post-mortem. It was unconvincing and he quickly drafted some questions for the defence counsel before leaving the court to attend a patient. When he returned the case had been concluded and the woman had been sentenced to death. He was assured that the bulk of the evidence had been damning but his doubts remained and he produced a written opinion that was passed to the judge. Mantell was then asked to look into the matter more closely. He established that the original tests had been inadequate to prove the presence of arsenic and, more significantly, he showed that no dose could have caused death within the time suggested by the prosecution. His opinion was supported by several eminent physicians and surgeons and on 26 February 1827 he was able to record in his journal that Hannah Russell had been pardoned and released as a consequence of his communication to the Secretary of State, Mr Peel. He then published a treatise on the medical evidence necessary to prove the presence of arsenic in cases of suspected poisoning.

Despite these distractions Mantell had been working on *Illustrations of the Geology of Sussex*, which deals with the fossils of the Tilgate Forest. It was written as a continuation or sister volume for *The Fossils of the South Downs* and is notable for having the first speculative description of the environment in which the dinosaurs lived.

In March 1829 he took a young partner to ease his medical workload and give himself more time for geology. He also turned part of his house into a museum. The idea was that it would only be opened on the first and third Tuesday of each month between 1 and 3 pm but this did not work out; visitors turned up at all hours and we can imagine that Mrs Mantell was not amused!

In 1831 Mantell wrote an article, *The Age of Reptiles*, which appeared in the *Sussex Weekly Advertiser* and was then reprinted elsewhere. He explained that reptiles had been the 'Lords of Creation' before the existence of the human race and several clergymen were deeply shocked as it challenged some of their beliefs.

Despite the renown that his discovery of Iguanodon had brought him, and his many other achievements, Mantell was a dissatisfied man and one of the saddest entries in his journal was penned on 3rd February 1830, his fortieth birthday. "How very little have I done, and how trifling my acquirements to what I had hoped to have attained long ere I reached this period of existence."

When William IV and Queen Adelaide visited Lewes in October 1830 their schedule was supposed to include a visit to Mantell's Museum but interminable civic ceremonial swallowed up too much of the available time. Mantell did, nonetheless, meet the king and presented him with a specially bound history of the town. Afterwards Mantell wrote an account of the visit but, to his disgust, hardly any copies were sold.

In 1833 Mantell decided to make the move to Brighton that he had long been contemplating and Lord Egremont, who was a generous patron of men of learning, gave him a thousand pounds to assist with the cost of the upheaval. In December the family left Lewes and moved into a house in the fashionable centre of Brighton. Mantell had high hopes of developing a more prestigious and profitable medical practice among the beau monde of Brighton but was to be disappointed. He was perhaps becoming too obsessed with his growing fossil collection, which occupied an entire floor of the house.

A few months after moving to Brighton Mantell acquired an impressive group of Iguanodon bones and teeth from a stone quarry at Maidstone. Embedded in a thick slab eight feet across there were fifteen vertebrae, several ribs and a variety of other bones. Up to that time his ideas about the appearance of Iguanodon had been highly speculative; these fossils enabled him to form a much more accurate idea of the size

Gideon Mantell in 1837
after a portrait by J.J. Masquerier

and appearance of the monster. The large rock containing these fossils was nicknamed the 'Mantell-piece' by his friends and can now be seen in the Natural History Museum. With thousands of fossils taking up ever more space the house was scarcely a home. Then in March 1836 he announced that he was going to let the house to the newly formed Sussex Scientific and Literary Institution and Mantellian Museum. He retained a parlour and a bedroom for himself but Mrs Mantell had to take the family back to Lewes, to a rented cottage at Southover. In August she returned to Brighton, settling in a cottage on Western Road but their marriage was on the rocks.

The Museum was well patronised and Mantell became a popular speaker but he was not making money and things could not go on as they were. He tried to raise funds by selling his collection to Brighton Council but they were not interested and shortly afterwards he opened negotiations with the British Museum. He also decided to buy a medical practice in the London area so that he could be closer to the nation's learned institutions and at the beginning of April 1838 he moved to Clapham Common.

In 1839 the British Museum purchased his collection for £4,000. It was a good price but he was displeased when he visited the Museum sometime later and found they had only put the Iguanadon and Hylaeolaurus bones on display. At about the same time Mrs Mantell effectively ended their marriage by moving to Devon along with their long-term housekeeper, Hannah Brooks. In September his daughter Ellen Maria left and within days his son Walter, who had just completed his medical apprenticeship in Chichester, sailed for New Zealand after refusing Mantell's offer of partnership. Only his daughter Hannah and youngest son Reginald remained. Hannah had been experiencing ill health for some years and was getting worse. In March 1840 she died. He felt her loss deeply and regularly visited her grave at Norwood Cemetery.

Mantell had by this date achieved international fame and was moving in distinguished circles but he never found the sense of achievement and satisfaction that he sought. His last years were spent in frustrating academic rivalry and his journal reveals a deal of bitterness.

In 1844 he moved house for the last time, to 19 Chester Square, Pimlico, and wrote in his diary that he faced the move "with a shattered constitution and without one kind heart to rest upon." He was experiencing severe pain from a spinal complaint that had bedevilled him since a carriage accident in 1841, but he refused to let it inhibit his activity. His journal shows that he was continually on the move as he always had been. After a trip, to Lewes in 1846, he indulged in a little uncharacteristic nostalgia and wrote *A Day's Ramble in and about the Ancient Town of Lewes*. He described places of interest in and around the town and touched on historical events like the Battle of Lewes in 1264 and events that he could recall like the avalanche of 1836. A poem by G.F. Richardson describing a ramble that Mantell led in 1836 was also included.

During these final pain racked years his geological research continued to be productive and he identified two more dinosaurs. Then, on 9th November 1852, he slipped on the stairs of his house and after crawling to his bedroom took a dose of opium to relieve his pain. It was not sufficient to be fatal under normal circumstances, but it proved too much for his exhausted body and he died on the following day. He was buried at Norwood Cemetery, beside his beloved daughter Hannah, and in accordance with his wishes the funeral was a simple affair to which nobody was invited.

ESTHER MEYNELL

Sussex Cottage, 1936.

Building a Cottage, 1937.

Sussex, 1947.

Small Talk in Sussex, 1954.

Esther Hallam Moorhouse was born in Yorkshire where her Quaker father had a large corn-milling business, the Concordia Mills at Leeds. When she was between eight and nine years old Esther suffered from something her doctors described as 'brain fever', probably meningitis, and was at death's door for several weeks. They concluded that she should not do schoolwork and over the years that followed she remained at home learning mainly what interested her, history and English literature.

When she was ten the family moved to Sussex and had a house built at Patcham, which was then a quiet rural village. Her father wanted to live somewhat like a smallholder keeping chickens and growing sufficient fruit and vegetables to be self-sufficient. While the house was being built her parents went abroad for a year, touring through France and Switzerland. Looking back Esther Meynell supposed that her parents had wanted a holiday free from family cares for she and her sister were left with a Mrs Browne, who lived with three unmarried daughters in a large semi-detached house at the Upper Drive, Hove. Mrs Browne, was none other than the widow of Hablot K. Browne, better known as 'Phiz', the famous illustrator of Dickens' novels.

The years that followed at Patcham were happy ones. In the winter there were outings to skate on Falmer pond and these excursions invariably included tea at a Miss Hogben's, which included eggs, hot buttered toast, honey from cottage hives and real Sussex fleed-cakes and plum-heavies. In summer they often went to the nearby country retreat of a Brighton architect and it was there that Esther first appreciated the beauty of the South Downs and sensed the brooding presence of Chanctonbury.

E.V.Lucas, who came from another Quaker family, occasionally called on the Moorhouse household at Patcham and encouraged Esther's literary inclinations. He told her to use plain Saxon English, to read Cobbett and *Lorna Doone* for examples of style and to write about simple things that she knew. She was an avid reader and after seeing an article about Thomas Hardy was keen to read some of his novels. Unfortunately, she found that her mother did not approve. She was told that his books were not nice and quite unsuitable for a young girl. Esther had to wait, but when she eventually read him she was enthralled; she saw that he spoke for a rural England that was dying, an England that she too loved.

Although she never went to school it was deemed appropriate that she should pursue some course of further education. She had shown an aptitude for drawing and was taken to the Brighton School of Art where she was asked to draw plaster casts of the Elgin marbles using chalk on grey paper. That seemed far too dull and she chose instead to enrol as a student at the Brighton School of Music. She did well as a pianist and won a scholarship entitling her to a year's free tuition. She also became familiar with the music of J.S. Bach, which became a lifelong passion.

Music took on a growing importance in her life but did not displace a long-standing interest in British naval history. This had started as an interest in Nelson but had broadened. She was keen to write about the subject and began by submitting a review of a naval book to the *Daily Chronicle*. She took care to sign herself simply as E. Hallam Moorhouse, for she guessed that her sex might put them off. The Literary editor, James Milne, replied explaining that they did not normally accept unsolicited contributions but that he would make an exception in this instance because the piece "showed such remarkable knowledge of naval affairs." Soon she was writing all their naval book reviews and it amused a friend of her family, who had some connection with the *Chronicle*, to tell them that E. Hallam Moorhouse was a crusty retired naval officer who scarcely ever spoke without swearing!

Later, when she wrote an article about Nelson for the *National Review*, the editor, who knew her, insisted on printing her full name. The staff of the *Chronicle* saw the article and the cat was out of the bag.

Fortunately, Milne saw the funny side and after meeting her decided to broaden her contributions to the Chronicle by asking for an article on 'Sussex in Summer'. Then he asked her to review the Sussex books of Kipling and Belloc. He seems to have sensed her attachment to the county. In due course Milne introduced her to Arthur Waugh and the firm of Chapman and Hall and she began to write books for them. The first under their imprint was *Samuel Pepys administrator, observer, gossip*, which came out in 1909 when she was eighteen.

In 1911 she was married at Patcham to Gerard Tuke Meynell, a nephew of Wilfred and Alice Meynell, who would one day become head of Westminster Press. They lived for a time in a small flat in Bayswater. Esther was not keen on urban life but took advantage of it by attending organ recitals, especially when she could enjoy the music of Bach. Their holidays were, of course spent in Sussex, mainly at Ditchling

When she was thinking of writing a novel about Bach's second wife, which eventually appeared as, *The Little Chronicle of Magdalena Bach*, she was afraid that she might make some glaring error when referring to organ music. She, therefore, decided to become more familiar with the instrument. She was already attending a series of Bach recitals that were being given at St Anne's, Soho, by Albert Orton, a Fellow of the Royal College of Organists and after one of the recitals she approached him. She explained, with some trepidation, why she wanted to know more about the organ and asked if he could give her some tuition. He was going away but agreed to give her six lessons when he came back. By the end of the six he recognised her musical ability and asked her if she wanted to continue. She did and the lessons went on for three years.

Throughout their time in London she and Gerard planned to move to Ditchling where they would either buy or build a cottage. "As a child I knew it," she wrote, "as my children have known it from their infancy. We have sojourned in half the houses it contains, from the picturesque inconvenient to the neatly modern." How the plan to settle there became a reality is described in *Sussex Cottage*, which was published in 1936. The book divides into four sections, the first of which is devoted to how their cottage was built. The other sections are 'Some Sussex Villages', 'Lewes and a Little Archaeology' and 'The South Downs.' Despite its title, *Sussex Cottage* is Esther Meynell's personal view of Sussex, which she summed up in the following sentence. "The sense of the past still broods visibly over this county which has never been a shire, but always a kingdom, complete in itself." Sussex Cottage came out in the same year as a plethora of other Sussex books including a new edition of *Highways and Byways in Sussex* by E.V. Lucas, *The County of Sussex* by Hilaire Belloc and *Sussex* by George Aitchison, but her very personal style made it distinctive.

She was delighted to be back in the Sussex countryside for she saw herself as a Sussex woman despite her Yorkshire birth. It was her instinct to stay at home and enjoy the place she had come to love. "Even in books" she explained, "I would rather read the history of an English farm, or a Bronze Age encampment on the South Downs, than of China or Peru." She loved everything about the local countryside and built up a collection of bygones that included harvester's bottles, Pycombe crooks, a canister sheep-bell and a pair of ox shoes.

After only five years they decided that the cottage was too big and Esther Meynell's next book, *Building a Cottage*, is a straightforward account of how a second, smaller, property was built. She was on site almost every day and chronicles everything that happened from the planning stage, which began on 14th January 1936, with a letter to the architect, right through to her moving in on 29th September 1936. The accommodation was modest but she was very particular about some points. She wanted to be able to see the South Downs when she was in bed and the living room had to have a large brick ingle fire-place, extensive book-shelving and space for her beloved Bluthner grand piano. All this was achieved and the book is illustrated with pencil drawings by the architect that show the result.

It was doubtless on the evidence of her descriptive writing in *Sussex Cottage* that Robert Hale commissioned her to write the first of their 'County Books' series, *Sussex*. Her approach was exemplary, she made no attempt to be comprehensive and wrote only about the parts of Sussex that she knew and loved best. *Sussex* came out in 1947 and was followed in 1954 by *Small Talk in Sussex*. In the latter she utilised material that had been inappropriate for the 'County Book' and the result is both more informal in structure and discursive in style. It is packed with out of the way information and I only wish that the publisher had taken the trouble to add an index.

THE REV. WILLIAM DOUGLAS PARISH
A Dictionary of the Sussex Dialect, 1875.

Many Victorian parsons with sparsely populated country livings had an abundance of leisure time which they could devote to whatever pursuits their inclinations dictated. In the case of the Rev. W. D. Parish, vicar of Selmeston, those interests were etymology and archaeology and he produced a notable Sussex classic, *A Dictionary of the Sussex Dialect,* which was published in 1875.

William Douglas Parish was born on 16th December 1833, son of a distinguished diplomat and naturalist, Woodbine Parish F.R.S., and his wife Amelia (Morse). Woodbine Parish, who was knighted a few years later, had been attached to Lord Castlereagh's staff when peace terms were negotiated following the overthrow of Napoleon and the treaty signed on the part of Great Britain in 1815 is in his handwriting. Later he served in Albania and then in South America where, despite a heavy political workload, he found time to indulge his interest in geology and palaeontology. William was born shortly after his father's return from Buenos Aires.

He was educated at Charterhouse and Trinity College, Oxford, and then served as a curate at the combined parishes of Firle and Beddingham from 1859 to 1863 before becoming vicar at Selmeston and Alciston, where he remained for 41 years.

His 500 or so parishioners still spoke in the drawling dialect of their forefathers pronouncing Selmeston and Alciston as 'Simpson' and 'Ahson' and he was fascinated by their colourful vocabulary. He recognised that they retained the most ancient forms of many words and that these had long since gone out of use in urban communities. He also realised that their distinctive provincial dialect was unlikely to survive the advances that were being made in education and decided to record any interesting words and phrases that he heard as he tramped around the area visiting the scattered homes of his flock.

It should not be thought that Parish's interests were solely academic;

he was also keen on cricket and both formed and coached a local cricket team.

From photographs we can see that Parish was a robust man with a firm chin and the testimonies of neighbouring parsons bear witness to his good-humour and popularity. The rector of nearby Berwick, the Rev. E. Boys Ellman, described him as one of the most genial of men he knew, an amusing conversationalist and a favourite with all classes. The Rev. A.A. Evans, vicar of East Dean with Friston, recalled that he had been an 'original' and declared that he "was like no one else of his time, certainly among the parsons of Sussex."

Ellman recorded several anecdotes about Parish in his *Recollections* and these throw further light on his personality. He tells us that Parish had plenty of money and that he could afford to go wherever he pleased when he chose to take a holiday. His taste in holidays was, however, eccentric. He chose to visit America, early in the early 1860s, at the time of the Civil War, just to see what was going on! Then, during the siege of Paris he developed a desire to go there and was only dissuaded by earnest entreaties from his father.

Another of Ellman's anecdotes concerns an occasion when he asked Parish, who was a confirmed bachelor, for a contribution to 'Clergy Widow's Fund'. Parish refused to subscribe, explaining that he was already helping by not getting married!

His sense of humour is equally apparent in his *Dictionary of the Sussex Dialect*, which the Rev. A.A. Evans rightly described as 'one of the most amusing as well as informing works of the county's literature'. In compiling it Parish built on earlier work by William Durrant Cooper and received over a hundred words from the Rev. J.C. Egerton, vicar of Burwash but its success was entirely his own achievement. Although he exercised proper academic rigour, the *Dictionary* was never aimed solely at specialists and his sense of humour is apparent throughout.

One of his most commonly quoted definitions is for the dialect word 'Adone'. He gives its meaning as 'Leave off' but goes on to explain that when a Sussex girl says "Oh! do adone," she wants you to continue whereas when she says "Adone do," you must stop immediately!

Similarly, having defined 'Concerned in liquor' as meaning 'Drunk' he adds a few supplementary comments including the following observation. "In the village of Selmeston the blacksmith's shop is next door to the public house. I have met numbers of people going to the forge, but never one going to the Barley-mow."

The book abounds with wonderfully expressive Sussex words like 'disremember', meaning 'forget', 'dracly-minute', meaning 'immediately' and 'dunnamany', meaning 'I don't know how many'. It also has words that reveal how local people viewed the world; the word 'foreigner' being used for anyone from another county. Those counties were spoken of as the 'Sheeres' but his definition of 'Sheeres' shows that its coverage was even wider. "The true Sussex man" he explains, "divides the world into two parts. Kent and Sussex form one division, and all the rest is 'The Sheeres'. I have heard China and Australia both described as in the sheeres." He also explains that 'Frenchy' was used for all foreigners who did not speak English and illustrates its usage by recalling a fisherman giving an account of a Swedish ship that was wrecked on the Sussex coast. The man finished by saying that "he thought the French Frenchys, take 'em all in all, were better than the Swedish Frenchys, for he could make out what they were driving at, but he was all at sea with the others."

In 1877 Parish was appointed Chancellor of Chichester Cathedral by Bishop Durnford and from then on he was generally known as Chancellor Parish. The workload associated with this post cannot have been particularly onerous for he continued to pursue his interest in dialect and archaeology with undiminished vigour.

He collaborated with the Rev. W.F. Shaw, vicar of Eastry in Kent, on the compilation of *A Dictionary of Kentish Dialect* and remained an active member of the Sussex Archaeological Society. On behalf of the latter he edited an impressive volume entitled *Domesday Book in relation to the County of Sussex*, which was published in 1886. The book comprised a facsimile of the Sussex portion of the Domesday Survey, an expanded version of the Latin text and a translation. At the time it was a landmark publication, but the translation has been superseded. In the same year he was elected to the Council of the Society and was chairman of the Council from 1895 to 1903.

One of Parish's friends of long-standing was Charles Dodgson, better known as 'Lewis Carroll'. Dodgson often stayed at the rambling Selmeston vicarage and it has been suggested that part of *Alice Through the Looking Glass* was written there, in a summer house in the garden. That is almost certainly a myth but there was a papier-mâché model of the 'Jabberwock' in the dining room. A granddaughter of the Rev, Edward Boys Ellman knew it well and later recalled that when she was a child she had "never tired of being told by Mr Parish how this creature had been the source of inspiration of one of Carroll's characters in *Alice*".

Parish died on 23rd September 1904 and was buried at Selmeston. His life had been lived largely in a quiet rural environment and had been uneventful but he is remembered for his *Dictionary*. Interest in it has never waned. An expanded and augmented version illustrated by Helena Hall was published in 1957 and, in 2001, Country Books published yet another edition with notes on the Sussex Dialect from *Highways & Byways in Sussex* by E. V, Lucas and 19th century line drawings by Frederick Griggs.

MAUDE ROBINSON
A South Down Farm in the Sixties, 1938.

Maude Robinson was born in May 1859 at Saddlescombe where her father, Martin Robinson, had a 900-acre farm. Her parents were both devout Quakers and the family travelled to Brighton twice a week to attend the Friends Meeting House in Ship Street. She was the youngest of eight children, those nearest to her in age being Ernest, who would one day take over the farm and Louis, who became a doctor. Her childhood was idyllic and she wrote an account of it that appeared serially in the *Sussex County Magazine* between May and September 1935. It was clumsily titled 'Child Life on the South Downs in the Sixties' and was followed in October by a piece titled 'School Life at Lewes in the Seventies.'

The articles attracted a good deal of interest and were noticed by the

Saddlescombe Farm in the 1860's

honorary editor of *The Friends' Quarterly Examiner*, a periodical to which she had already contributed. He suggested that she should 'Quakerize' the narrative, dwelling on the aspects of her childhood that would be of most interest members of their denomination. She did so and then adapted the narrative again, this time for publication in book form. *A South Down Farm in the Sixties* was issued by J.M. Dent & Sons in 1938 and a 2nd impression followed in 1947. The first paperback edition came out nearly half a century later, in 1994, with the revised title *Quiet Valley, Memories of a South Down Farm in the 1860s*.

When she was a child the Saddlescombe farm supported 900 sheep that were divided into three flocks. They were folded on arable land by night, but each flock roamed the downland by day followed by its shepherd and his dog. She recalled that the shepherds were a race apart in those days and that two of them, Thomas Shepherd and Fred Wooler, had names which suggested that their ancestors must have followed the calling for centuries. She also described how oxen were still used for ploughing when she was young. They were paired by size so that the wooden yokes might be level; then one of the pair would be given a name with a single syllable and the other a name with two. Thus, typical names were 'Quick and Nimble', 'Crisp and Curly' and 'Peart and Lively'. Although the book provides many interesting insights into agricultural practices she also explains what home life was like on a farm in such a secluded situation.

In 1872 Maude Robinson went to a private boarding school at Lewes. It was run by three Quaker ladies, the Misses Mary and Catherine Trusted and Miss Rachel Special, who dressed in the primmest gowns and addressed their pupils as 'thee' and 'thou'. The school regime was Spartan but the mistresses were kindly and a good education was provided.

One by one the older Robinson children moved away from Saddlescombe farm until, after the death of her parents, only Ernest, who ran the farm, and Maude remained. Both of them loved the downland and took an interest in its wildlife. Maude Robinson also kept bees as a profitable pastime, made character dolls that she sold in order to raise money for charities and wrote both articles and short stories. The collections of short stories that were written at Saddlescombe are *The Time of her Life*, 1919, *Nicholas the Weaver*, 1922, and *Wedded in*

Prison, 1925. They were written for children and almost every tale illustrates a Christian virtue. In the preface to the first book she explains that various family relics made her curious to find out what she could about her ancestors and it was these researches that provided many of the ideas for her stories. Most of the stories are rich in Sussex colour and have some basis in historical fact.

Maude Robinson aged 80 in 1939

Ernest died in 1925 and Maude then moved to 11 Windlesham Gardens, Brighton, where she continued to write producing another volume of short stories and several magazine articles. *The King's Reward*, came out in 1938 with a title story about Charles II's escape after the Battle of Worcester. The hero is Dick Carver, a Quaker who was mate aboard Nicholas Tettersell's coal-brig *Surprise*, the ship that carried the king from Shoreham to France. As with her earlier collections, many of the tales have Sussex settings and one, 'Serviceable on Truth's Account', includes passages from letters that were written by Miss Robinson's great-great-grandfather.

Many of Miss Robinson's later articles reflect her interest in the flora of the South Downs and were contributed to the *Wild Flower Magazine*. Others that appeared in the *Sussex County Magazine* include 'Weeds found in Sussex' (November 1939), 'Reptile Neighbours of the South Downs' (December 1942), and 'Wild Life on the South Downs' (July and August 1946).

Her Christian faith and her Quaker principles remained firm to the end, which came in 1950.

GEORGE FORRESTER SCOTT
[John Halsham]

Idlehurst: A Journal Kept in the Country, 1898.

Lonewood Corner: A Countryman's Horizons, 1907.

Old Standards: South Country Sketches, 1913.

George Forrester Scott was a shy scholarly man who, although he lived quietly and comfortably in pleasant surroundings, was deeply pessimistic. The world around him was changing and he hated what was happening. He believed that speculative building was defiling the landscape and that school standards and other London influences were steadily eroding all traces of local character. "London airs" he wrote, "blow into the smallest village in Arcadia."

George Forrester Scott was born in 1863, the eldest son of Benjamin Forrester Scott, of Oulton, Yorkshire, and later of Wilmington, Kent. He was educated privately in Surrey and at St Mary College, Oxford. After taking his degree he went to art school for a spell and then settled at the Manor House, Lindfield, which now known as Old Place. It is a delightful gabled property situated near to the church and was his home for eleven years. Afterwards he moved just a few miles north to Lywood House at Ardingly, where he remained for the rest of his life. He lived an almost reclusive life but enjoyed participating in some local activities, like bell-ringing, and, during the First World War, overcame his shyness sufficiently to become secretary of the East Sussex Sailor's and Soldier's Association and to organise a rifle range. He was a regular contributor to *The Times* and the *Times Literary Supplement*, an occasional contributor to the *Saturday Review* and the author of a number of books. He wrote under the pseudonym, John Halsham, a name that appealed to him because his Kentish ancestors had intermarried with the Halshams of West Grinstead during the 15th century.

He wrote his first book, *Idlehurst: A Journal Kept in the Country*, while he was at Lindfield and it was published in 1898. The 'journal' provides a series of vignettes describing life in Lindfield, which he disguises by calling it 'Arnington'. He describes his garden, the village and the neighbouring countryside and introduces us to several local characters: Henery Bish, his gardener, 'Muster' Lewknor, the Rector, Phineas Tomsett, an octogenarian labourer, Dr Culpeper, Kitty Culpeper and many more. It is a closely observed picture of Wealden life at the end of the nineteenth century.

Lonewood Corner, A Countryman's Horizons was written a decade later, after Scott had moved to Lywood House. It deals with life in Ardingly, which he calls 'Sheringham', and is similar to the earlier book in style and content. He was still despondent at the way the countryside and country life were changing but he expressed some satisfaction at having discovered that the process of change was less advanced at Ardingly than it had been at Lindfield! In this volume we are introduced to an entirely new community of characters including the Misses Louisa and Fanny Walcot, who live next door at 'The Laurels', Mrs Ventom who runs Burntoak farm with benevolent tyranny, the Warden of the local Almshouse, who occasionally accompanies the author on his walks, and the Warden's charming niece Molly Crofts.

His next book, *Old Standards: South Country Sketches*, is a collection of essays that had first appeared in the *Saturday Review* and is a worthy companion volume for *Idlehurst* and *Lonewood Corner*.

Scott is remembered mainly for the three books mentioned above but he also wrote a gardening manual for townsfolk moving to the country and one novel, *Kitty Fairhall*. He set *Kitty Fairhall* in the familiar surroundings of Ardingly, which he calls Ashfield, and he includes scenes at Ousebridge (Lewes) and Ousehaven (Newhaven), but the novel is disappointing. It has only one memorable character and the plot, which is rather thin, develops at a snail's pace.

Scott's main pleasures were the enjoyment of his garden at Lynwood House, walking and reading. He loved his books and chapter XXII of *Lonewood Corner* is a eulogy on the subject of his library. His own taste was for the Greek and Latin classics and he declared that he got "more pleasure from the dead languages – spite of the drag of an inveterate hobble in construing – than from any other form of reading". He spent most of his evenings reading the Greek poets and almost invariably devoted his Sunday afternoons to reading from his most treasured volume, a Venetian edition of Dante's *Divina Comedia* dated 1568. He read it so often that he almost knew it by heart. When he died from angina in 1937 his obituary in *The Times* was headed 'The Perfect Countryman' and he was summed up in the following terms. "He was steeped in all the lore of the English countryside and was the master of a singularly pure and beautiful literary style, formed and strengthened by his life-long love of the classics."

SIR CHARLES THOMAS-STANFORD

Sussex in the Great Civil War and the Interregnum 1642-1660, 1919.

Wick, A Contribution to the History of Hove, 1923.

The Private Memorandums of William Roe of Withdean, 1928.

Charles Thomas was born at Highgate in London in 1858, the eldest son of David Collet Thomas, a ship'-owner and shipbroker. His mother Anne (Lloyd) came from Denbigshire and many of his childhood holidays were spent at his grandfather's home in that county. At ten he went to Highgate School and in the following year won a scholarship that provided exemption from school fees. By the end of his school days he was Head Boy and had won, in addition to many other prizes, the Governor's Gold Medal for Latin Verse and an open scholarship at Oriel College, Oxford. His academic success continued at Oxford where he also excelled at sport becoming captain of the Oriel Boat Club and rowing in the University Trial Eights.

While he was at Oxford he got to know Cecil Rhodes, one of the college alumni who invariably visited the university when he was in England, and Thomas was destined to meet him again in Africa.

After graduating Thomas read for the Bar and was called in 1882 but never practised, preferring to join a shipping firm in the city. After two years he moved to his father's firm and then, in 1890, went into partnership on his own account. He was, however, more interested in literature, history, travel and sport and gave up the partnership in 1894. In the following year he made his first visit to South Africa.

At the end of 1895, after an arduous journey from Bulawayo, Thomas arrived in Johannesburg on Christmas day and was there to witness the outcome of the ill-judged and rashly executed Jameson Raid. Jameson invaded the Boer Republic of the Transvaal on December 29th with just 500 Rhodesian troopers expecting the Uitlanders (non-Boers), who formed the majority in Johannesburg, to rebel. Instead the raid turned into a fiasco and Jameson had to surrender on 2nd January 1896. Thomas made notes about all that he saw and later published a brief account of the affair. Later in the year, when the Matabele were in revolt, Thomas and a companion set out with only one native guide to join Cecil Rhodes, who was camped in the bush. They discovered that he had moved and were distinctly concerned for their safety until they found the new encampment and saw Rhodes in a canvass chair, calmly reading Gibbon's *Decline and Fall of the Roman Empire*. It was a work that he took with him wherever he went.

Thomas returned to England for a spell but was back in Africa by the autumn. At the end of the year he sailed for home and broke his journey at Madeira where he met Ellen Benett-Stanford, the only surviving daughter of William Stanford of Preston Manor, Brighton, and widow of Vere Fane Benett-Stanford M.P. They were married in 1897 and, in accordance with the wishes of Ellen's father, Thomas adopted the name Stanford. He also quartered the Stanford arms with those of his own family by Royal licence.

Although Thomas-Stanford's parents were both of Welsh stock his connections with Sussex did not begin with his marriage. His Thomas grandmother had lived in Brighton for some years before her death and both his parents and his Lloyd grandparents had settled in Hove. After a few years in London the Thomas-Stanfords made their home at Preston Manor, but usually took a fishing holiday on the Gaula River in Norway during the summer and spent part of every winter at Quinta Stanford in Madeira where their garden became a showpiece. Two of Thomas-Stanford's early books reflect these interests, namely, *A River in Norway: Being the Notes and Reflections of an Angler* (1903) and *Leaves from a Madeira Garden* (1909). He also wrote an indifferent thriller, *The Ace of Hearts*, which he set in Madeira.

Having settled in Brighton Thomas-Stanford became involved in local affairs becoming a Councillor and Alderman and serving as Mayor for three years. In 1914 he was returned as Member of Parliament for the town and served until 1921. He also took an interest in the history of Preston Manor and the Brighton area. He joined the Sussex Record Society in 1901 and the Sussex Archaeological Society in 1904; becoming chairman of the latter's Council from 1920 to 1929. He had just become chairman when the society was given an opportunity to buy

Lewes Castle and he was able to curtail plans for fund raising by announcing that he would buy it and present it to the society as trustees for the nation.

The most significant book that he wrote was *Sussex in the Great Civil War and the Interregnum 1642-1660*, a work of great scholarship. In its preface he explains that it was really the outcome of a lecture he delivered at Brighton Public Library in November 1909 under the auspices of the Sussex Archaeological Society. It was suggested that the lecture should be printed but he concluded that a mere leaflet would be inappropriate for so large a subject and decided to research the topic more fully. The result was *Sussex in the Great Civil War*, which was described (in volume 73 of the *Sussex Archaeological Collections*) as the "model of what such a book should be, scholarly without being pedantic, giving due emphasis to local events without forgetting the greater happenings in other places, written in a clear and lucid style, attractive to the general reader without being merely popular, and marked throughout by breadth of view and a deep interest in the subject."

Wick, A Contribution to the History of Hove is a much slimmer volume. It is simply a paper that he read before the Brighton and Hove Archaeology Society along with a supplementary note correcting misconceptions about the manor of Hove, which had been inaccurately described by successive historians including Horsfield and Lower.

The Private Memorandums of William Roe of Withdean in the County of Sussex 1775-1809 is another slim volume. The 'private memorandums' are, in effect, the diary of a successful Civil Servant who bought an estate at Withdean and their main interest lies in the information they provide about the history of the Withdean area of Brighton.

Sir Charles Thomas-Stanford c.1929

Thomas-Stanford was an ardent

collector of early printed books and built up one of the finest collections in the country. It included several early editions of Euclid and an illustrated monograph describing them was published by the Bibliographical Society. He also collected books by Sussex authors and had numerous editions of the John Selden's works. His most treasured volume was one of these; a copy of Selden's *Mare Clausum* of 1635 that had been owned by Archbishop Laud and had the Archbishop's arms on its cover.

Over the years he received many honours. He was elected a Fellow of the Society of Antiquaries in 1906, he and his wife were made Freemen of the Borough of Brighton in 1925 and two years later he received the Honorary Degree of Doctor of Literature from the University of Wales. Finally, in 1929, he was made a Baronet for "public services in Brighton and district." He died in March 1932 and left Preston Manor to Brighton Corporation to serve as a museum of local antiquities, subject to the life interest of his wife who died before the year was out.

THOMAS TURNER

The Diary of Thomas Turner, 1754-1765 (1984)

The diary of Thomas Turner of East Hoathly is a Sussex classic because it provides such a uniquely vivid picture of life in a Sussex village in the eighteenth century. It is also important for the light it throws on how tradesmen did business at that time. It was written in at least 116 notebooks of which 111 survive and it covers more than a decade, beginning with an entry for 21st February 1954.

Thomas Turner was born in 1729 at Groombridge in Kent but the family moved to Sussex when he was five; his father having taken a shop at Framfield. In 1750, when he was just twenty-one, Thomas took over the business of a mercer in the nearby village of East Hoathly and three years later married Margaret (Peggy) Slater, whose parents were farmers at Hartfield. The diary opens five months after their marriage when his wife was going through a difficult pregnancy.

At that time East Hoathly was a village of around sixty houses and seventy-five families. It was a village like any other but was notable for having Halland House, the principal seat of Thomas Pelham-Holles, Duke of Newcastle, within the parish boundary; Newcastle being prime minister (First Lord of the Treasury) for much of the period covered by the diary. Most of the villagers were employed in agriculture but there were two publicans and a number of tradesmen. Socially, the leading villager was the wealthy rector, the Rev. Thomas Porter. There were land-owning gentry nearby, other than the Duke of Newcastle, but they lived some way off, on their estates. The villager who owned the most property, including a number of farms, the mill and the forge, was a widow, Mrs Elizabeth Browne and Jeremiah French was the most prosperous of the nearby farmers. East Hoathly is still a village, although it had grown, and Turner's long, low house is still there, although it has been divided into three cottages.

Turner was a successful businessman who traded in just about anything that his village community required. He dealt with several fairly local suppliers; buying, for example, hats from John Jenner of Hailsham, clay pipes from Thomas Harman of Lewes, and beehives from Thomas Burfield of Steyning. He sold rags to Edward Blackwell, a papermaker at Hawkhurst in Kent and bought paper from him. He also dealt with several London firms and with haberdashers in Manchester. He knew how to turn a profit but was forever grumbling about trade. On 20th August 1756 he wrote: "Oh, how dull is trade, and how scarce is money!" An almost identical entry was made a few months later on December 16th and similar sentiments recur throughout the diary.

Turner's primary occupation was shopkeeper but the shop was not his only source of income. He was a general factotum who was often called upon to write up accounts, draw up inventories, write petitions and draft wills. For some years he was the local collector of land and window taxes, which entitled him to 3d in every £1 he collected, and for one year he ran the village school. As a schoolmaster he may well have been popular with his pupils for on his birthday he treated them to 5 quarts of strong beer and on another occasion he hired an itinerant fire-eater to entertain them!

He was also a conscientious parish officer serving at different times as churchwarden, overseer of the poor and surveyor of the highways.

Turner's principal leisure interest was reading and he sometimes wondered if he was unduly self-indulgent in this respect. On 23rd March 1758 he wrote: "I believe [that] by a too eager thirst for knowledge I have…been at too great an expense in buying books and spending rather too much time in reading, for it seems to be the only diversion that I have any appetite for." He certainly read both a great many and a great variety of books. He read classical works like Homer's *Odyssey*, translated by Pope, novels like Richardson's *Clarissa*, which he found unduly prolix, Shakespeare's plays, collections of sermons, technical books, journals and newspapers.

Turner also enjoyed sport. In the summer he liked to watch cricket matches and sometimes played. He mentions several matches played between rival village teams and others that were purely local to East Hoathly, played, for example, between tradesmen and farmers (23rd September 1756) or between married men and bachelors (25th June 1763). Sometimes just four men would play for a small wager. His diary entry for 28th June 1763 describes one such match: "In the even Joseph

Fuller and myself played a game of cricket with Mr Geo. Banister and James Fuller for half a crown's worth of punch, which we won very easy. But being hot, and drinking a pretty deal of punch, it got into my head; so I came home not sober..." Other sports that get a mention are horse races at Lewes and cockfighting at village inns.

Parties were part of the social round for Turner's set in the village. The entertainment usually began with tea and card games. They played brag for money and could win or lose a few shillings. This would be followed by a hearty supper and then the revelry really began. The following is from Turner's entry for 7th March 1758 and describes how matters proceeded after a supper at Joseph Fuller's. "There we continued drinking like horses (as the vulgar phrase is) and singing till many of us was very drunk, and then we went to dancing and pulling off wigs, caps and hats. And there we continued in this frantic manner (behaving more like mad people than they that profess the name of Christians)..." Similar revelry had already occurred at Jeremiah French's on 22nd February and would be repeated at the Rev. Thomas Porter's on 10th March and then at Turner's house on the 14th. After the latter event he expressed the hope that all the revelling for the season was over!

Turner's main preoccupations may have been parochial but he kept abreast of national affairs. He was interested in the fate of Admiral Byng after the loss of Minorca in 1756 and believed that he should not have been executed. In his journals for 1759 he mentions newspaper reports of a string of British military successes. On 9th July he was relieved to read that the threat of a French invasion had been removed by Admiral Rodney's destruction of troop transports at Le Havre. On 20th October he read with delight that General Wolfe had defeated the French at Quebec and on 8th December he joined in the general rejoicing to celebrate Admiral Hawke's success at Quiberon Bay. There was a bonfire and a discharge of cannon in the grounds of Halland House, and a "considerable quantity of beer [was] given away among the populace." Afterwards Turner enjoyed a supper of cold roast beef with several villagers, including the rector, and drank more loyal toasts than he could handle. "I came home about 11.15" he noted, "after staying in Mr Porter's wood near an hour and a half, the liquor operating so much in the head that it rendered my legs useless."

Early in the diary we learn that Turner's home life was not as happy as he would have wished. His wife, Peggy, was quarrelsome and although a son was born in August 1754 he proved sickly and died only a few months later. Rows with his wife were frequent until she became seriously ill towards the end of 1760. Over the weeks that followed Turner repeatedly noted that she was in continual pain and by April 1761 he knew that she was dying. On June 17th the rector administered communion and on June 23rd she died. She had been at odds with Turner throughout their marriage but he missed her sorely.

A few years later he got to know Mary (Molly) Hicks of Chiddingly and in March 1765 he described her as his favourite girl. He also commented on her good sense and good nature and observed that he found her both discreet and prudent. By April 14th he is describing her as his "intended wife" and on June 19th they were married. Turner had already lost interest in his diary but made a final entry on July 31st to record his marriage and his optimism. From that day on he was either too busy or too contented to reopen his diary but we know that the couple had seven children and that the business continued to prosper. On 1st October 1766 Turner was able to buy his shop and on 28th February 1772 he bought the *King's Head* public house. He died in 1793, aged sixty-three, and is buried in the churchyard at East Hoathly.

His diary first came to the attention of the public in 1859 when R.W. Blencowe and Mark Anthony Lower selected extracts for publication in volume 11 of the *Sussex Archaeological Collections*. Turner's grandson had lent the diary to them but they failed to recognise its importance and their main objective in publishing extracts was to highlight how life had changed for the better since Turner's day. As a result, they were highly selective. The diary entries that appeared in the article attracted a good deal of interest and were quoted in several subsequent publications, perhaps most extensively in *Glimpses of our Sussex Ancestors* (1882) by the Brighton newspaper proprietor Charles Fleet. Then, in 1925, a small volume entitled *The Diary of Thomas Turner of East Hoathly* was published with a foreword by Turner's great-great-granddaughter, Florence Maris Turner Lamb and an introduction by J.B. Priestley. Unfortunately, it comprised no more than the extracts that Blencowe and Lower had selected. These were re-issued without the original commentary and without appreciating that some of the entries had been quoted out of chronological order. Nobody had consulted the original notebooks, although they were available, having been deposited with the Sussex Archaeological Society at Barbican House in Lewes.

In 1944 the diaries were acquired by Yale University and shortly afterwards became the subject of research projects by Harold P. Melcher Jr. and Dean K. Worcester Jr. The latter wrote an important monograph, *The Life and Times of Thomas Turner of East Hoathly*, in which he drew attention to the limitations and shortcomings of the above mentioned publications, but decades would pass before a satisfactory edition of the diaries was published.

A corrected version of the original extracts was issued in 1979 as *The Diary of a Georgian Shopkeeper*, with an introduction by G.H. Jennings, but the most extensive and best edition of the diary was published in 1984 under the title *The Diary of Thomas Turner, 1754-1765*. It was edited by David Vaisey and, as he explains in his preface, it was produced after revisiting the original manuscript. Only a third of Turner's text has been used but it gives a more representative impression of the diary and the omissions consist mainly of reflections on moral issues, trivial financial transactions and details of meals that would have proved repetitive if they had been treated exhaustively.

Turner was by no means the only Sussex diarist and anyone who is interested in the others should consult *Old Sussex and her Diarists* (1929) by Arthur J. Rees or relevant volumes of the *Sussex Archaeological Collections*. Of particular note are the seventeenth and eighteenth century diaries of Giles Moore, Rector of Horsted Keynes (*S.A.C.* vol. 1, 1848, pp.65-127), of Timothy Burrell, barrister, of Ockenden House, Cuckfield (*S.A.C.* vol.3, 1850, pp.117-172), of Walter Gale, schoolmaster at Mayfield (*S.A.C.* vol. 9, 1857, pp.182-207) and of Thomas Marchant of Little Park, Hurstpierpoint (*S.A.C.* vol.25, 1873, pp.163-203)

BARCLAY WILLS

Bypaths in Downland, 1927.

Downland Treasure, 1929.

Shepherds of Sussex, 1938.

Barclay Wills was born a Cockney but he was a countryman at heart and came to know the shepherds of the South Downs better than anyone else of his generation.

Harry Barclay Wills was born in Islington on 22nd June 1877 and seems to have been known to his family as Harry although he never used the name for his books. Barclay was his mother's maiden name. His father and grandfather had clerical positions in publishing and in due course he too became a clerk. He hated the work and looked forward to any spare time that allowed him to get away. He was then living in Highgate, and would go to open spaces like Hampstead Heath or the nearest countryside. On a few occasions he went further afield to the New Forest and the Isle of Wight. "I only survived," he later explained, "by earning a reputation for eccentricity, for my sketch-book and binoculars saved me from the hopeless futility of suburban life." Many of his drawings of birds and plants from this period survive and they show that he was a talented artist.

In 1905 he married Bertha Paddock and within three years they had moved a short distance to Fortis Green, another London suburb, where their daughter Mollie was born. As a child she would accompany him on several rambles and she features in his first book as 'Daphne', which must have been her pet name.

Barcaly Wills had his first sight of Sussex when he went to stay with a friend at Frant, near Tunbridge Wells and he later recalled an incident that occurred when they were out walking. After ascending a bank, his friend beckoned him over to a gap in a hedge. "Look through there," he said pointing airily at a panoramic view that left Wills spellbound. "That, my boy, is Sussex! There is enough stuff there to last all your life."

He knew that his friend understood his interests and must have taken the comment to heart for he remembered it and eventually realised his dream by moving to Brighton, probably in 1922. At first he and Bertha ran a small general store at 50 Lavendar Street, Kemp Town, an area that must have seemed just as suburban as north London, but the South Downs were nearby and they were the attraction. For some reason the shop did not work out and by January 1924 they had taken on the Willow Café on Dyke Road. Then, before the year was out, they moved to 59 High Street, Worthing where they kept a grocery shop for four years. The next venture was another grocery shop, this time in the village of Durrington, and in 1932 they moved to yet another at 1 Brougham Terrace, Brougham Road, East Worthing, where they lived above the shop. We can guess that Barclay Wills was no more interested in being a shopkeeper than he had been in being a clerk. The advantage was that he could slip away to the Downs when business was slack and leave things to his wife.

After settling in Sussex one of his earliest rambles took him to Falmer where he came upon a flock of sheep and lambs and heard to sound of sheep bells for the first time. He was captivated and spoke to the shepherd, Nelson Coppard. It proved to be an important meeting for they got on well and were destined to become close friends. The immediate rapport that developed between them was remarkable for the downland shepherds were solitary men who had little time for strangers; it tells us a good deal about the unassuming personality of Barclay Wills.

He began to learn about shepherding from Nelson Coppard and their friendship became his passport when he met other shepherds. One by one they got to know and trust him. They told him about their lives and added to his collection of sheep bells and other shepherding gear.

Another man he met at this time was John Pull, a postman and amateur archaeologist who was interested in the prehistoric flint mines on the Downs near Worthing. He and Barclay Wills also became firm friends and Pull soon found that Wills had a particularly sharp eye for surface finds. In an article on Stone Age villages that was published in the *Sussex County Magazine* he mentions how patiently and successfully Barclay Wills searched the fields between High Salvington and Church Hill, gradually building up an impressive collection of flint implements.

The Society of Downsmen was founded soon after Barclay Wills arrived in Sussex and he became one of the first members in January 1924. It had been founded to stimulate interest in the South Downs and campaign for their preservation, and Barclay Wills did his bit. He served on committees and was, for a time, the district officer responsible for keeping an eye on the downland near Worthing. In the latter capacity he warned the Society in 1929 of a proposed housing development close to Cissbury Ring and it was successfully averted. The society also brought him into contact with a number of men he would not otherwise have met, including Arthur Beckett, newspaper proprietor and author of *The Spirit of the Downs*, Dr. Habberton Lulham, poet and photographer, and Robert Thurston Hopkins, author and journalist. They all became his friends and encouraged him to write.

His first book *Bypaths in Downland* was published in 1927, and gives an account of his rambles on the Downs. Each chapter is complete in itself and the following are typical headings: 'A Dewpond Chapter', 'The Green Hairstreak Butterfly', 'Cissbury Ring in June', 'Downland Sheep Bells' and 'Findon Fair'. It is in this book that we learn how he met Nelson Coppard and we are introduced to many other shepherds. It is illustrated with some of his own bird drawings and several photographs that he took with a Kodak 'Brownie' box camera. His style is unpretentious, almost conversational, and when I put this book down I am invariably left with the feeling that I have been listening to Barclay Wills.

Downland Treasure followed in 1929 and is similar in format and content. In the very first chapter he observes that the older shepherds are dying out and wistfully observes that their history has yet to be written. "It was kindly suggested" he continues, "that I should undertake the task; but, alluring as the subject is, I have found it impossible to comply with the request. Like many other alluring things, the whole matter is one of pounds, shillings and pence. A poor man cannot afford to do it."

Arthur Beckett was the man who had made the 'kindly suggestion' and he was unimpressed by these protestations. When he reviewed the book for the October issue of the *Sussex County Magazine* he declared that Barclay Wills was talking nonsense. "The only qualities required are patience, perseverance and the knowledge which Mr Wills himself possesses. Mr Wills has the ability to write; he is an excellent artist, both with pencil and camera, and he has immense sympathy with his subject. If he does not write the book which he can write better than any other man he will fail to do himself justice." This was a public challenge that Wills could scarcely ignore and happily he did eventually write the book.

Shepherds of Sussex appeared serially in Arthur Beckett's *Sussex County Magazine* during 1933, but was not published in book form until 1938. Methuen's had published his previous books when their chairman was E.V. Lucas, a Sussex enthusiast, but he was dead and the market for Sussex books was being overwhelmed. When it ultimately appeared Arthur Beckett forecast that it would become a Sussex classic and his expectation has been fulfilled. For many years copies were much sought after on the second-hand market and were difficult to obtain; now, happily it is in print again having been reissued by Country Books in 2001.

In around 1935 Wills met Nancy Price, a well-known actress and author who contrived to spend some of her time away from the limelight in a cottage near High Salvington Mill. She called at the shop on Brougham Terrace to make some purchases and only then discovered that its softly spoken proprietor shared her love of the Downs. They became firm friends. He visited her and they went for downland walks together.

In 1938 he developed a chest complaint and a young policeman was asked to convey him to the General Hospital. By some happy chance that policeman was Bob Copper, who would himself become a writer on downland lore. He was impressed by the quiet dignity of the patient and found that they were kindred spirits with common interests. He visited Barclay Wills at the hospital and continued seeing him after he had been discharged. He was shown round Wills' den, which was a mini-museum of shepherding gear and flint tools, and Wills presented him with copies of his books. It was yet another example of the knack that Barclay Wills had for making friends.

In the following year, shortly before the outbreak of war, the family moved to 57 Ham Road, East Worthing. The war years were difficult, business was bad and his recurrent chest complaint began to inhibit his rambling.

After the war he concentrated his efforts on 'flinting', which he once described as the cheapest of all hobbies. He was interested in any flint implements that he could find but was most keen on 'eoliths'. Because they are the oldest and crudest stone tools 'eoliths' are the most difficult to identify and some archaeologists, like Eliot Curwen, viewed his conclusions with scepticism. Wills described his 'flinting' in the manuscript for a fourth book, *Discoveries in Downland*, but never found a publisher. Little can have seemed to go well during those post war years for he was distressed that large tracts of downland were being turned over to agricultural use, he continued to suffer with bronchitis and his precarious financial situation showed no sign of improving. Finally, knowing that neither his wife nor his daughter had any interest in his collections he began to dispose of them. The end came on 1st April 1962 and he was cremated.

Nancy Price was among the few who recognised his genius and it was through her persistence that an exhibition in his memory was mounted at Worthing Museum in May 1963. He nonetheless remained comparatively unknown and much that we now know about Barclay Wills is the result of painstaking research carried out by Shaun Payne when he was teaching at Windlesham House School near Findon. He had become enthusiastic about the work of Barclay Wills after reading *Bypaths in Downland* and went on to edit an anthology of his writing, *The Downland Shepherds*

VISCOUNTESS WOLSELEY

Some of the Smaller Manor Houses of Sussex, 1925.

Sussex in the Past, 1928.

Some Sussex Byways, 1930.

Frances Garnet Wolseley was born in Pimlico in 1872, the daughter of Colonel Garnet Wolseley (later Field-Marshall Viscount Wolseley) and his wife Louisa (Erskine). When Wolseley joined the army he believed that the fastest path to promotion would be for him to try to get killed whenever he had an opportunity and it worked. He fought with distinction in the Second Anglo-Burmese War, the Crimea War and the Indian Mutiny and after surviving several wounds with only the loss of an eye became, at the age of 25, the youngest Lieutenant-Colonel in the army. When Frances was born he had just been appointed assistant Adjutant-General at the War Office but much more active service lay ahead including the Ashanti Expedition of 1873-4 and his victory at Tel-El-Kabir in 1882.

One inevitable consequence of her father's career was that Frances never put down roots. In *Myth and Memory* she comments on this. "I once counted how many houses my parents had lived in from the time of my birth until I started housekeeping in a humble way on my own account. Including only those houses that we had owned or had been tenants of for a whole year at a time the number was thirteen."

She also recalled that she was quite a small child when she first longed for a home in Sussex. Her first memories of the county were of holidays spent at a cottage near Midhurst. When they were there she used to roam round Cowdray Park in the care of her mother's maid or ride her pony through the sunken byways of Lodsworth, Tillington and Fernhurst, accompanied by her father. Later they spent a year at a Manor House near Haslemere and explored the wooded countryside north of Blackdown. From her room she could see Chanctonbury on the distant skyline. It was while she was there that she first took an interest in gardening. When the gardener, was mowing she used to help him by sweeping leaves from the lawn and emptying the box of grass-cuttings. "He was typical of Sussex," she later wrote, " a man of slow decision; but, when he did take a line of his own, he stuck to it."

The family was living at Rangers House, Blackheath, when her schoolroom days began to draw to a close and her mother advised her to find a hobby that could hold her interest into later life. She chose gardening and was given responsibility for their home garden. As she knew very little about the subject she subscribed to a gardening paper that was edited by William Robinson and asked a few questions through its columns. He answered them and afterwards they began to correspond by letter. He was struck by her enthusiasm and invited her, and her mother, to see his garden at Gravetye Manor, West Hoathly, in East Sussex. The visit was a success, they found the Elizabethan Manor house and its garden enchanting, and were impressed by their tall black bearded host, who became a lifelong friend.

Two years later Frances and her mother became acquainted with another gardening enthusiast who lived in East Sussex, Charles Eames Kempe, an artist whose speciality was stained glass. He lived at Old Place, Lindfield and they were often his guests. At the time he was extending his picturesque 16th century timber-framed house and redesigning the garden. The development of the garden was one attraction but Frances also liked to take her horses so that she could enjoy gallops on the Downs.

Like every other aristocratic young lady, Frances was presented at court and enjoyed a whirl of balls and social functions during the London season. She was also very much a countrywoman who loved both hunting and taking long solitary walks with her dogs.

Early in 1898 the Wolseleys rented Glynde Place from friends for just a few months and so liked it there that they decided to take a dower house in the grounds. It was known simply as Farm House and was a happy choice; it gave Frances ample scope to enjoy riding, walking and gardening.

In 1903 her mother saw an advert placed by a lady gardener who was in 'distressed circumstances' and engaged her. Her employment then sparked the idea of founding a school for lady gardeners and by March their first students had enrolled. More followed in April and Frances was sufficiently encouraged to take an acre of glebe land at the bottom of the village. The villagers were highly amused by the idea of women gardeners but came round to the idea when they found that the students were willing to pay well for board and lodgings.

The project attracted interest at home and abroad and Frances was sufficiently encouraged to draw up a proper prospectus and invite friends who were well known in gardening circles to be patrons. These included Gertrude Jekyll and William Robinson. By 1906 it was apparent that she would need more land and she rented five and a half acres called Ragged Lands, where a cottage was built for her head gardener. The sloping site had dreadful chalky soil but it caught the sun and was protected on the north side by Mount Caburn. In 1907 she took over the cottage and set up house on her own for the first time. It was no easy matter to transform Ragged Lands into a garden but she was undaunted and she succeeded brilliantly.

Her father died in 1913 and by a special remainder she succeeded to his titles. Thereafter she was a Viscountess in her own right. In the same year she was admitted to the freedom of the City of London through the Worshipful Company of Gardeners in recognition of her services to agriculture and her pioneer work in developing gardening as a respectable occupation for young women.

In 1914 she handed her College of Gardening over with all profits to a former pupil, Miss Elsa More, who had been working as her 'foreman'. She then engaged in a variety of voluntary wartime activities and had two books published, *In a College Garden* and *Women and the Land*, which both came out in 1916. In 1917, the Board of Agriculture appointed her to a post that involved organising women's work on the land in East Sussex. To assist her she took on a secretary, Mrs Musgrave, whose husband was then on active service. They became close friends and she would later refer to Mary Musgrave as her outspoken friend 'Bimbo'. Viscountess Wolseley had too much initiative for the Board of Agriculture and in September she was told that they really wanted someone more humble and amenable. She accordingly resigned and went to live with Mary Musgrave at Ditchling. They spent some time considering what use they could make of their experience, especially in support of the war effort, and decided to run a smallholding with the object of demonstrating how much food-stuff they could produced on a small acreage.

In January 1918 they received details of Massetts, an Elizabethan house near Scaynes Hill, and it seemed to meet all their requirements. They took it on a twenty-one year lease and moved in eight weeks later. Lady Wolseley continued writing and *Garden Design* was published in 1919. It was followed in 1921 by a very different work called *A Countryman's Log Book*, which deals with country life. Inspired by her curiosity about Massetts she became particularly interested in old houses and her next book was *Some of the Smaller Manor Houses of Sussex*. It was well received and when Arthur Beckett founded the *Sussex County Magazine* in December 1926 he asked her to contribute a series entitled 'Historic Houses of Sussex'. Over the years that followed she described 115 houses, the last 4 articles appearing posthumously. In *Myth and Memory* she declared that she would always be glad that she had been chosen to write the series for it enabled her to spend her summers exploring the county she loved looking at fascinating houses. In winter she did her research.

She liked the idea that Massetts was tucked away "amidst farms and unfrequented lanes" but its isolation was also a drawback, in a way that neither she nor Mary Musgrave had anticipated. Maids did not want to work a half-hour's walk from the nearest shop, far from a bus route and farther still from a railway station. After seven years Lady Wolseley decided that the time had come to find a smaller house near to a bus route. It had to have modern conveniences like electricity, mains water and central heating and along with all of these there had to be a glorious view. She feared that it might be too much to hope for, but in 1925 she found an ideal site at Ardingly. It overlooked the Weald facing south where the pale blue outline of the South Downs was visible in the distance. She had a house built to her own specifications and called it

'Culpeper's' because that family had once owned the land. At the same time Mary Musgrave moved into Upper Lodge Cottage an adjacent property.

At about the time of her move to Ardingly a room was built onto Hove Public library at her expense to house books on agriculture and horticulture. Later the library received her collection of documents, photographs, postcards, engravings and other records of notable Sussex houses. Today the room houses a Sussex and local history collection.

It was after settling at Culpeper's that she wrote *Sussex in the Past*, which I consider to be her finest book. It only concerns a small area, the Hundred of Steyning, in the Rape of Bramber, but what an area this is, comprising such villages as Coombes, Botolphs and Washington and that iconic landmark Chanctonbury Hill. Her stated object was that her readers should gain some impression of the "unchanging peace and restfulness which still exists for those who really know the outlying, remote parts of our Downland and Wealden countryside." The book was published by the Medici Society and is an attractive volume. The paper is of high quality, the top edges are gilt and it has eight superb colour illustrations by Garnet R. Wolseley.

Her next book, *Some Sussex Byways*, is similar to *Sussex in the Past* in format and style but she ranges far and wide across the county in search of interesting byways. Her last book was a small volume of essays, *Myth and Memory*, published in 1934. In a chapter entitled 'Sussex' we learn how she came to know and love the county and in 'My Garden' she explains how she developed her garden at Culpeper's.

A severe muscular illness inhibited her mobility during her final years but she embarked on a book of reminiscences that was to be called *Silhouettes from Memory*. It was never published in its entirety but was utilised by her biographer, Marjory Pegram.

Lady Wolseley died on Christmas Eve 1936 and was buried at Beddingham, where she had worshipped in the days when she lived at Ragged Lands.

GERARD YOUNG

Chronicle of a Country Cottage, 1940.
Come into the Country, 1943.
The Cottage in the Fields, 1945.
Down Hoe Lane, 1950. A History of Bognor Regis, 1983.

During the nineteen thirties books about people settling in Sussex cottages almost became a distinct genre. The early books of Gerard Young fall into this category but stand out from the run of these publications. They have a freshness because he simply described things as they were and events as they happened, without trying to fit them into a hackneyed image of rural Sussex.

Gerard Donovan Young was born at Leigh-on-Sea, Essex in 1912, but his parents moved to Worthing in 1918 and he grew up there with his sister, Patricia, and brother, Derek. He enjoyed family picnics on the Downs at High Salvington, Lancing Clump, Kithurst Hill and elsewhere and these engendered a lifelong love of the West Sussex countryside. He went to two local preparatory schools and then to a Jesuit school, Beaumont College, Windsor, from 1926 to 1930. While he was there he began writing short tales about the South Downs and these were published in the *Sussex County Herald*. He also developed an interest in theatre and took part in school plays. When he was on holiday he haunted Worthing's cinemas, the Winter Hall, Picturedome, Dome and Rivoli, and filled notebooks with comments on the films that he saw.

He trained for the theatre at Swiss Cottage and had ambitions to be a producer, but concluded, after joining the Gaumont-British Film Company, that he was more suited to writing and moved to their publicity department. In the course of his work he got to know many stars including Maureen O'Sullivan, the first Jane in the Tarzan films, and Robert Donat, the romantic hero of films like the 1935 Alfred Hitchcock version of *The Thirty Nine Steps*. Some became his friends and their pictures, neatly bound in passe-partout, later adorned the walls of his Sussex cottage. After a few years he left the film world to become a publicity agent for Jessie Matthews and Sonnie Hale at the peak of their stage careers.

Although he lived in London and sometimes went on tour with musicals he developed the habit of taking weekend breaks at Flansham, and friends would join him there. He, of course, knew the area well but the specific attraction of Flansham was its guest'-house, Flansham Manor, which was run by Mrs Jacks. His visits became an important part of his life and he was taken aback when he learned in 1937 that she was going to let the property. He realised that he could not bear to lose his links with Flansham or with people like Mrs Jacks and the family of farmer Owen Adames, who were his closest friends. Mrs Jacks suggested that he should think about taking Meadow Cottage, which was lying empty and he took a look at it. It lay down Hoe Lane, a deep sunken cart track, and its entrance was a gap in the high bank flanked by rotting gateposts. The gate had long since fallen into a bramble bush. He climbed the bank and looked around.

"From the edge of the bank a level field ran back northwards towards the Downs. A good way back from the top of the bank there was a barbed wire fence separating the half-acre in which we stood from the rest of the virgin meadow. This was the 'garden'. And plumb in the middle of this rectangle of untouched land was the ugly, red-brick, tiled-roof, bungalow that boasted the picturesque name of Meadow Cottage."

The story of how he took the cottage, made it habitable, and constructed a garden is told in *Chronicle of a Country Cottage*. We are introduced to several villagers and it makes an entertaining tale. Young was not a naïve man but he was apparently surprised when he found that people who had enjoyed the book were seeking out the village so that they could take a look at it. He also found that many other readers were writing to him on gardening questions, having assumed that he was an expert!

Come into the Country followed in 1943 and is somewhat different in character. Month by month it takes us through a year in the village. It has some wonderful descriptive passages and several diversions into local history. The villagers also feature prominently. His first book was illustrated primarily with photographs but *Come into the Country* has 24 of Young's own drawings including a superb fold-out bird's eye view of Flansham. One cannot help wondering what the villagers thought about having an account of their lives published, but at least one of them co-operated. Week by week Young read each newly written chapter to Jack Adames so that he could check the accuracy of any agricultural details.

The third in the series, *The Cottage in the Fields*, continues the saga, while incorporating observations on the 3 years that William Blake, poet, painter and mystic, spent at Felpham and devoting part of another chapter to the story of a remarkable local building, Bailiff's Court at Clymping. Young was deeply interested in local history and belonged to the Sussex Archaeological Society. He counted S.E. Winbolt, author of *With A Spade on Stane Street* (1936), among his closest friends and assisted him of a number of digs. On one occasion Winbolt gave him some Roman tiles. "Romans made them for their Sussex homes," he said, "why not keep using them?" Young agreed and they were incorporated into the garden paths at Meadow Cottage. Winbolt was addicted to sending postcards with cryptic messages and Young received one when his first book was published. "Am glad you keep yourself within sound simple language," he wrote, "not indulging in that high falutin' nature nonsense which has often made me nearly puke in reviewing country books."

The last of Young's 'cottage books' was *Down Hoe Lane*, which came out in 1950 and comprises a collection of pieces, most of which had originally appeared in the Glasgow Evening News. I think it is the least satisfactory of the books but it is the one that turns up most regularly in second hand bookshops.

When he decided to spend all his time in Flansham Young joined *The*

Bognor Post and used to cycle back and forth with a cigarette dangling from the corner of his mouth. His weekly column became an important feature and through it he stimulated a great deal of interest in local history. He kept up involvement with theatre by producing plays for a local amateur group, *The Barnstormers*, and by advising the West Sussex Council's drama school at Lodge Hill. To his colleagues he was a man of many contradictions, stubborn but charming, sometimes dour but possessed of a keen sense of humour, a bit of a loner but wonderful company. They remembered him as a great, if enigmatic, character and a first class journalist.

After a long illness he became a patient at University College Hospital, London, on 1st January 1972. A few weeks later he was transferred to his mother's home in Kensington and died shortly afterwards.

Over the years Young had collected a considerable file of source material relating to the area and had been preparing *A History of Bognor Regis* when he died. The work was quite advanced and his brother Derek, who was also a journalist and a member of the Bognor Regis Local History Society, undertook its completion. It was published by Phillimore in 1983 and is now regarded as the definitive local history.

BIBLIOGRAPHY

Arthur Beckett (1871-1943)
    Spirit of the Downs — 1909
    The Wonderful Weald — 1911
    Adventures of a Quiet Man — 1933
Hilaire Belloc (1870-1953)
    Sussex Painted by Wilfrid Ball — 1906.
    The Four Men — 1912.
    The County of Sussex — 1936.
N.P. Blaker (1835-1920)
    Sussex in Bygone Days — 1919.
E. Cecil Curwen (1895-1967)
    Prehistoric Sussex — 1929.
    The Archaeology of Sussex — 1954.
Howard Dudley (1820-1864)
    Juvenile Researches — 1835
    The History and Antiquities of Horsham — 1836
Tickner Edwardes (1865-1944)
    An Idler in the Wilds — 1906.
    The Bee-Master of Warrilow — 1907.
    Neighbourhood — 1911.
    A Downland Year — 1939.
J. Coker Egerton (1829-1888)
    Sussex Folk and Sussex ways — 1884.
Edward Boys Ellman (1815-1906)
    Recollections of a Sussex Parson — 1912.
A.A. Evans (1862-1946)
    On Foot in Sussex — 1932.
    A Saunter in Sussex — 1935.
    By Weald and Down — 1939.
Thomas Geering (1813-1889)
    Our Parish: A Medley — 1884.
    Our Sussex Parish — 1925.
John Halsham (1853-1937)
    Idlehurst — 1898.
    Lonewood Corner — 1908.
T.W. Horsfield (1792-1837)
    History and Antiquities of Lewes &c. — 1824-27.
    History, Antiquities and Topography of the County of Sussex — 1835.
W.H. Hudson (1841-1922)
    Nature in Downland — 1906.
Richard Jefferies (1848-1887)
    Nature near London — 1883.
    The Life of the Fields — 1884.
    The Open Air — 1885.
    Field & Hedgerow — 1889.

Mark Anthony Lower (1813-1876)
    Contributions to Literature — 1854.
    The Worthies of Sussex — 1865.
    A Compendious History of Sussex — 1870.

Richard Lower (1782-1865)
    Stray Leaves from an Old Tree — 1862.

E.V. Lucas (1868-1938)
    Highways and Byways :In Sussex — 1928.

Gideon Algernon Mantell (1790-1852)
    Fossils of the South Downs — 1822.
    Illustrations of the Geology of Sussex — 1827

Esther Hallam Meynell (1890-1955)
    Sussex Cottage — 1936.
    Building a Cottage — 1937.
    Sussex — 1947.
    Small Talk in Sussex — 1954.

W.D. Parish (1863-1904)
    A Dictionary of the Sussex Dialect — 1875.

Maude Robinson (1859-1950)
    A Southdown Farm in the Sixties — 1938.

George Forrester Scott (1853-1937) [See John Halsham,.]

Sir Charles Thomas-Stanford (1858-1932)
    Sussex in the Great Civil War and the Interregnum — 1919.
    Wick, A Contribution to the History of Hove — 1923.
    The Private Memorandums of William Roe of Withdean — 1928.

Thomas Turner (1729-1793)
    The Diary of Thomas Turner 1754-1765. — 1984.

Barclay Wills (1877-1962)
    Bypaths in Downland — 1927.
    Downland Treasure — 1929.
    Shepherds of Sussex — 1938.

Frances, Viscountess Wolseley (1872-1936)
    Some of the Smaller Manor Houses of Sussex — 1925.
    Sussex in the Past — 1928.
    Some Sussex Byways — 1930.

Gerard Young (1912-1972)
    The Chronicle of a Country Cottage — 1940.
    Come into the Country — 1943.
    The Cottage in the Fields — 1945.
    Down Hoe Lane — 1950.
    A History of Bognor Regis — 1983.

SOURCES

Abbreviations: DONB = Dictionary of National Biography
SRS = Sussex Record Society
SAC = Sussex Archaeological Collections
SL = Sussex Life.
SCM = Sussex County Magazine.

General: Author's & Writer's Who's Who, 1948-9.
Smith, Bernard & Peter Haas, *Writers in Sussex*, 1985.
O'Neill, Martin, West Sussex Literary, Musical & Artistic Links, 1996.

Arthur Beckett (1871-1943)
Eastbourne Gazette, 12 May 1943.
SCM vol.1, 1927, pp.82-5. [*The Society of Sussex Downsmen and its Activities* by R. Thurstan Hopkins.]
SCM vol.10, 1936, pp.535-9. [*Sussex Books of Arthur Beckett* by Gilbert Pass.]
SCM vol.17, 1943, pp.121-2. [*The Death of our Editor* by A.E. Beckett.]
SCM vol.17, 1943, pp.156-7. [*A Personal Appreciation* by Gilbert Pass.]
SCM vol. 30, 1956, pp.249 & 297.[*County Notes* & poem by W.G. Daish.]
The Times, 13th April 1956, p.12. [Demise of Sussex County Magazine.]

Hilaire Belloc (1870-1953)
Copper, Bob, *Across Sussex with Belloc*, 1994.
Harrison, David, *Along the South Downs*, (1958) 1975, p.237.
Meynell, Esther, *Sussex Cottage*, 1936, p.186.
SCM vol. 27, 1953, pp.576-9. [*He Chose Sussex* by John Wright.]
SCM vol. 30, 1956, pp.320-3. [*The Bellocs in Slindon* by Josephine Rees.]
SL vol. 2, no.8, 1966, pp.30-1 [*The Path of the 4 Men* by Charles Tully.]
Speaight, Robert, *The Life of Hilaire Belloc*, 1957.
Wilson, A.N., *Hilaire Belloc*, (1984) 1997.

Nathaniel Payne Blaker (1835-1920)
Blaker, N.P., *Sussex in Bygone Days*, 1919.
Lucas, E.V., *Reading, Writing and Remembering*, 1932, pp.161-4.
The Times, 16th June 1920, p.19. [Will.]
Gilbert, Edmund W., *Brighton, Old Ocean's Bauble*, pp.190-1.

E Cecil Curwen (1895-1967)
Brandon, Peter, *The South Downs*, 1998, pp.34-7.
SCM vol. 4 ii, 1930, p.569. [*Sussex from the Air* by E. Cecil Curwen.]
SCM vol. 16, 1942, pp.190-4. [*Secrets of Thundersbarrow* by G.P. Burstow.]
SCM vol. 29, 1955, p.57. [*County Notes*.]
Sussex Notes & Queries, vol. 16, 1963-7, pp.357-8. [Obituary.]

Howard Dudley (1820-1864)
Dudley, Howard, *The History and Antiquities of Horsham*, 2002, [With an introduction by Dick Richardson utilising research by Brian Slyfield.]
Gentleman's Magazine, January 1865, pp.101-102.
Lower, M.A., *The Worthies of Sussex*, 1865, p.339.
SCM vol. 22, 1948, pp50-52. [*Juvenile Researches, or the Diligent Dudley* by Joyce Glover.]

Tickner Edwardes (1865-1944)
    Powys, John Cowper, *Autobiography*, (1934) 1994, pp.318-20 & 361-2.
    SCM vol. 1, 1927, pp.102-5. [*A Parson-Novelist at Home* by S. Russell Goggs.]
    SCM vol. 10, 1936, pp.181-4 & 255-9. [*The Sussex Books of Tickner Edwardes* by G. Pass.]
    SCM vol. 19, 1945, pp.32-5. [*Tickner Edwardes, A Memoir of Nature's Essayist* by A.B. Richards.]
    SCM vol.19, 1945, pp.244-5. [Obituary.]
    The Times, 30th December, 1944, p.6. [Obituary.]

John Coker Egerton (1829-1888)
    Hopkins, R. Thurston, *Kipling's Sussex*, (1921) 1924, p.32.
    Wace, Henry, *In Memoriam-John Coker Egerton*, from the Guardian, 18/4/1888, reprinted in the 1892 edition of J.C. Egerton's *Sussex Folk and Sussex Ways*.
    Wells, Roger, ed., Victorian Village. *The Diaries of the Reverend John Coker Egerton of Burwash, 1857-1888*, 1992.

Edward Boys Ellman (1815-1906)
    Ellman, Edward Boys, *Recollections of a Sussex Parson*, 1912.
    SCM vol. 30, 1956, p.335-7. [*Ellman of Berwick* by Stanley Godman.]

A.A. Evans (1862-1946)
    SCM vol.3, 1929, p.427. [*County Notes & News.*]
    SCM vol.10, 1936, p.739. [*Countryman's Diary* by the Rev. A.A. Evans.]
    SCM vol.20, 1946, p.108. [*Death of the Rev. A.A. Evans.*]
    SCM vol.20, 1946, p.154. [*The Rev. A.A. Evans: A Tribute* by E. Shoosmith.]
    SCM vol.24, 1950, pp.541-2. [*An Old Photograph* by W.H. Camplin.]

Thomas Geering (1813-1889)
    Beckett, *The Wonderful Weald*, (1911) 1924, pp.97-109.
    Geering, Thomas, *Our Sussex Parish*, 1925.

John Halsham, [See George Forrester Scott.]

T.W. Horsfield (1792-1837)
    Connell, J.M., *The Story of an Old Meeting House*, (1916) 1935, pp.81-99.
    Holman, George, *Some Lewes Men of Note*, (1905) 1927, pp.65-7.
    Lower, M.A., *The Worthies of Sussex*, 1865, p.331.
    Brent, Colin, *Georgian Lewes 1714-1830*, 1993, pp.108, 128, 155 & 201.
    Farrant, John H., *Sussex Depicted*, SRS, Vol. 85, 2001, pp.27-71.
    SAC vol.138, 2000, pp.234-5. [*Why did Horsfield leave Lewes?* By J. Goring.]

W.H. Hudson (1841-1922)
    DONB.
    Roberts, Morley, *W.H. Hudson. A Portrait*,1924.
    Haymaker, Richard E., *From Pampas to Hedgerows and Downs*, 1954
    Looker, S.J., ed., *William Henry Hudson A Tribute by Various Writers*, 1947.
    SCM vol. 2, 1928, pp.301 & 305. [*Where W.H. Hudson Stayed* by A.M. Adams.]
    SCM vol. 15, 1941, pp.242-3. [*County Notes.*]
    The Times, 19th August 1922, pp.11 & 13.
    Tomalin, Ruth, *W.H. Hudson*, 1982.

Richard Jefferies (1848-1887)
    Besant, Walter, *The Eulogy of Richard Jefferies*, 1888.
    Hudson, W.H., *Nature in Downland*, 1906, pp.14-7.
    Jefferies, Richard, *The Story of My Heart*, 1883.
    Keith, W.J., *Richard Jefferies a Critical Study*, 1965.
    Looker, S.J., ed., *Richard Jefferies A Tribute by Various Writers*, 1946.
    Middleton, Judy, *A History of Hove*, 1979, pp.185-6.
    SCM vol. 10, 1936, pp.322-4. [*Richard Jefferies in Sussex.*]
    SCM vol. 11, 1937, pp.524-30. [*Richard Jefferies and Sussex* by A. Anderson.]
    SCM vol. 22, 1948, pp.236-8. [*The Sussex of Richard Jefferies* by A. Sharp.]
    SL vol. 3, No. 9, Sept., 1967, pp.22-4. [*A return to Richard Jefferies' Goring* by Eric Joyce.]
    Thomas, Edward, *Richard Jefferies*, (1909) 1978.
    Concerning Richard Jefferies by Various Writers, 1944.

Mark Anthony Lower (1813-1876)
    Holman, George, *Some Lewes Men of Note*, (1905) 1927, pp.74-7.
    SAC vol. 27, 1877, pp.132-151. [Obituary.]
    SAC vol. 85, 1946, pp.11-15. [Biographical details in *A History of the Sussex Archaeological Society* by L.F. Salzman.]
    SCM vol. 20, 1946, p.190. [*A Sussex Wayfarer's Diary* by John Donne.]
    SCM vol. 22, 1948, pp.388-90. [*Mark Anthony Lower, Schoolmaster and Antiquary* by G. Mitchell.]
    SL vol.12, No.3, March 1976, pp.24-5.[*The Mark Anthony of Sussex* by John Wright.]

Richard Lower (1782-1865)
    Evans, A.A., *On Foot in Sussex*, 1933, pp.182-188.
    SAC vol. 27, 1877, pp.134-5.
    SL, vol.1, No.6, October 1965, pp.38-9. [*Sussex Dialect Poet's Centenary* by John Wright.]

Edward Verrall Lucas (1868-1938)
    DONB
    Lucas, Audrey, *E.V. Lucas A Portrait*, 1939.
    Lucas, E.V., *Reading, Writing and Remembering*, (1932) 1933.
    Lucas, *The Old Contemporaries*, 1935.
    Meynell, Esther, *A Woman Talking*, 1940, pp.25-7.
    SCM vol. 5, 1931, p. 379. [*Modern South Saxons.*]
    SCM vol.12, 1938, p. 495. [*The Sussex side of E.V. Lucas* by A. Beckett.]
    SCM vol.12, 1938, p. 512. [*Countryman's Diary* by the Rev. A.A. Evans.]
    SCM vol.22, p.70-2.[*County Notes.*]
    The Times, 10th February 1938, p.10. [Letter.]
    The Times, 27th June 1938, p.16. [Obituary]

Gideon Algernon Mantell (1790-1852)
    Cadbury, Deborah, *The Dinosaur Hunters*, 2000.
    Curwen, E. Cecil, ed., *The Journal of Gideon Mantell*, 1940.
    Dean, Dennis R., *Gideon Algernon Mantell and the Discovery of Dinosaurs*, 1999. [Dean had access to much hitherto unutilised material and this the most reliable biography of Mantell.]
    DNOB
    Gentleman's Magazine, December, 1852, pp.644-5.

Lower, M.A., *The Worthies of Sussex*, 1865, pp.158-9.
SCM vol.8, 1934, pp.566-7. [*Men of Sussex no.8.*]
SCM vol.11, 1937, pp. 118-122. [*A Case of Circumstantial Evidence* by Sidney Spokes.]
Taylor, James, ed., *The Sussex Garland*, 1851. [Includes poems by Mantell.]

Esther Hallam Meynell (1890-1955)
    Meynell, Esther, *A Woman Talking*, 1940.
    SCM vol. 11, 1937, p.270. [*Modern South Saxons.*]
    SCM vol. 29, 1955, p.131. [*Death of Mrs Esther Meynell.*]
    The Times, 7th February 1955, p.10. [Obituary.]

William Douglas Parish (1863-1904)
    Ellman, E.B., *Recollections of a Sussex Parson*, 1912, pp.209 & 239-41.
    SAC vol. 85, 1946, pp. 36 & 60-1.
    SCM vol.12, 1938, pp.132-5. [*A Countryman's Diary* by A.A. Evans.]
    SCM vol. 29 pp.154 & 251. [References to the Lewis Carroll.]
    SCM vol. 30, 1956, p.10& 12. [*The Voice of Sussex* by W.G. Daish.]
    The Times, 14th January 1932. [Letter from Rev. F.S. Morgan re 'Jabberwock'.]

Maude Robinson (1859-1950)
    SCM vol.13, 1939, p. 286. [*Modern South Saxons.*]
    SCM vol. 16, 1942, pp.122-3. [*County Notes.*]

George Forrester Scott (1863-1937) [pseudonym John Halsham.]
    SCM vol. 11, 1937, p.271. [*County Notes.*]
    SCM vol. 16, 1942, p.92-3. [*County Notes.*]
    SCM vol. 22, 1948, p.147-150. [*John Halsham Country* by Arthur Wilde.]
    The Times, 16th April 1937, pp.16. [Obituary.]

Sir Charles Thomas-Stanford (1858-1932)
    Jennings, Sir Arthur, *Sir Charles Thomas-Stanford, An Appreciation*, 1932.
    SAC vol. 85, 1946, pp.43-5, 120 & 122.
    SAC vol. 73, 1932, pp.lxvi-lxxi. [*Obituary.*]
    SCM vol. 3, 1929, pp.203 & 206. [*Modern South Saxons.*]
    SCM vol. 6, 1932, p.204. [*County Notes.*]
    The Times, 8th March 1932. [Obituary.]

Thomas Turner (1729-1793)
    Fleet, Charles, *Glimses of Our Sussex Ancestors*, 1882, pp.30-51.
    Jennings, G.H., ed., *The Diary of a Georgian Shopkeeper*, 1979.
    SAC vol.11, 1859, pp.179-220. [*Extracts from the Diary of a Sussex Tradesman a Hundred Years Ago* by R.W. Blencowe & M.A. Lower.]
    SCM vol.9, 1935, pp.546-550. [*Turner Trove* by L.B. Smith & E.A. Hadley.]
    SCM vol.25, 1951, pp.183-186. [*Diary of a Draper* by Garth Christian.]
    Vaisey, D., ed., *The Diary of Thomas Turner*, 1754-1765, 1984.
    Worcester, Dean K., *The Life and Times of Thomas Turner of East Hoathly*,1948.

Barclay Wills (1877-1962)
    SCM vol.3, 1929, p. 696. [Review of *Downland Treasure* by A. Beckett.]
    SCM vol.16, 1942, pp.96-99 & 146. [*Recent Finds of Palaeoliths in the Worthing Area* by F.W,H. Migeod and letter from Eliot Curwen.]

Payne, S. & R. Pailthorpe ed., Wills, Barclay, *The Downland Shepherds*, 1989.
[See Introduction by Shaun Payne & Foreword by Bob Copper.]

Frances, Viscountess Wolseley (1872-1936)
Pegram, Marjory, *The Wolseley Heritage*, 1939.
SCM vol. 3, 1929, p.670. [*Modern South Saxons.*]
SCM vol. 4, 1930, p.23. [*The Preservation of Old Sussex Deeds*
by Viscountess Wolseley.]
SCM vol. 11, 1937, pp.71 & 76. [Obituary & Appreciation.]
SCM vol. 20, 1946, p.268-72. [*Viscountess Wolseley: Herself and Her Books*
by Beryl Netherclift.]
SCM vol. 27, 1953, p.228 etc. [*Frances, Viscountess Wolseley*
by Beryl Netherclift.]
SL vol.8, No. 2, Feb., 1972, pp.55-7. [*The Wolseley Library, Hove* by J. Dove.]
Wolseley, Viscountess, *Myth and Memory*, 1934.

Gerard Young (1912-1972)
Bognor Post, 19 February 1972, p.7. [Gerard Young.]
SCM vol.18, 1944, pp.66-8. [*S.E. Winbolt: A Tribute* by Gerard Young.]

ENVOI

When I embarked on this book I declared that I would exclude living authors but it seems inappropriate to conclude these sketches without mentioning one or two current writers. Bob Copper immediately springs to mind as one of them for I cannot imagine a collection of Sussex books without his masterpiece, *A Song for Every Season* (1971). It tells the story of three generations of his family and takes us through the agricultural year with a feast of recollections before concluding with a selection of old country songs. The Coppers are, of course, famous for their singing and Bob Copper has done much to ensure that many of our traditional songs are not lost.

Bob Copper was born in Rottingdean in 1915 and, after leaving school, began work as a 'lather-boy' in a barber's shop. He went on to be a labourer, a trooper in the Life Guards and a West Sussex policeman before taking over a social club at Peacehaven. It was before his retirement that he began to write and *A Song for Every Season* won him the Robert Pitman literary prize in 1971. He was also voted Country Book Author of that year. Since then he has been awarded an honorary Master of Arts at the University of Sussex.

Bob Copper's other titles include *Songs and Southern Breezes* (1973), *Early to Rise* (1976, an account of his boyhood, *Across Sussex with Belloc* (1994) and *Bob Copper's Sussex* (1997). In addition to his books there are LP recordings and a CD with songs that he, his father, his Uncle John, and cousin, Ron, originally recorded for the BBC in the fifties.

Tony Wales, a lifelong Horsham man, has even more Sussex titles to his credit, over thirty at the last count, and like Bob Copper has a deep interest in song. He was the press and publicity officer for the English Folk Dance and Song Society and edited its magazine up to 1978. His books include *We Wunt be Druv* (1976), a collection of songs and stories from Sussex, and *A Sussex Garland* (1979), a nostalgic and light-hearted collection of rhymes, recollections and recipes.

It seems appropriate to finish with an anecdote that was recently related to me concerning the lady who was to become his stepmother. She attended the same Catholic church as that giant among Sussex writers, Hilaire Belloc and the incident is yet another illustration of the great writer's eccentricity. One Sunday morning Belloc came into the church with G.K. Chesterton and paused by the pew in which she was sitting. He then leaned across declaring "Madam, you are sitting in my seat!"

INDEX OF SUSSEX PLACE-NAMES

Adur	87, 107	Hartfield	94
Alciston	80	Hastings	55
Alfriston	43, 44, 58, 61	Horsham	23, 24, 25
Ardingly	87, 107	Horsted Keynes	98
Arundel	26, 39, 46	Hove	9, 20, 21, 22, 55, 75, 91
Beachy Head	7	Hurstpierpont	19, 98
Beddingham	34, 108	Kingston	15, 65
Berwick	36-38, 81	Lewes	16, 17, 21, 35, 36, 46, 47, 59, 60, 68, 69 72, 88, 92, 95, 98
Bognor Regis	111, 112		
Brighton	7, 9, 17, 18, 35, 46, 55, 56, 64, 72, 76, 84, 86, 91, 92, 100	Lindfield	87, 88, 105
		Lyminster	29
Brightling	14, 46	Mayfield	14, 98
Broadwater	53	Midhurst	23, 104
Burpham	26, 27, 28, 29	Newhaven	88
Burwash	30-33, 41	Pagham	42
Chichester	21, 23, 41, 46, 52, 82	Patcham	65, 75
Chiddingly	58, 61, 63, 97	Peacehaven	7
Clymping	111	Petworth	23
Chanctonbury	76, 104, 108	Pevensey	39
Crowborough	57	Plumpton	21
Cuckfield	70, 98	Portslade	15
Devil's dyke	8, 20	Robertsbridge	13
Ditchling	77-8, 106	Rotherfield	57
Duncton	14	Ripe	58
Easebourne	23	Saddlescombe	84, 85
Eastbourne	6, 22, 40	Salvington	64, 102, 109
East Dean	39, 40	Selmeston	15, 80, 83
East Hoathly	58, 94-98	Seven Sisters	8
Edburton	8, 15	Shipley	12
Falmer	75, 100	Shoreham	15, 49, 50
Felpham	111	Slindon	11, 12
Fernhurst	104	Slinfold	39
Findon	103	Southwick	20
Firle	34, 80	South Harting	7, 14
Fittleworth	67	Steyning	95, 108
Flansham	110-112	Thundersbarrow	20
Framfield	94	Ticehurst	43
Friston	9, 39	Tillington	104
Folkington	29	Washington	14, 108
Fulking	15, 16	West Grinstead	87
Glynde	34, 105	Worthing	49, 52, 55, 100, 101, 103, 109
Goring	51, 56		
Hailsham	43, 44, 63, 95		

OTHER SUSSEX TITLES FROM COUNTRY BOOKS
Available from all good bookshops, or in case of difficulty, post free from the publisher.

THEY WROTE ABOUT SUSSEX
A collection of biographical sketches
Richard Knowles
Paperback 210 x 148mm   126 pages. Illustrated by the author
ISBN 1 898941 81 5   Price **£12.50**

SUSSEX IN FICTION
Richard Knowles
The number of novels that are at least partly set in the county continues to rise, but in most cases the local background is purely incidental to the narrative. This book identifies those for which Sussex settings have some real relevance. About the authors and how they were connected with the county.
Paperback 210 x 148mm   194 pages Illustrated by the author
ISBN 1 898941 82 3   Price **£18.00**

OUR SUSSEX PARISH
Henry Geering
Introduction by Richard Knowles
A new edition including an extra story
ISBN 1898941 831
In preparation– date and price to be announced

Facsimile
SMUGGLING AND SMUGGLERS IN SUSSEX
'A gentleman of Chichester'
The murders of Mr William Galley, a customs house officer, and Mr Daniel Chater, a shoemaker, fourteen notorious smugglers, with the trials and execution of seven of the criminals at Chichester 1748-9. The sermon preached in the Cathedral Church at Chichester, at a special Assize held there, by Bishop Ashburnham; also an article on 'Smuggling in Sussex' by William Durrant Cooper, Esq., FSA (reprinted from volume X of the Sussex Archaeological Collections) and other papers.
Hardback 185 x 125mm   280 pages Engravings
ISBN 1 898941 61 0   Price **£20.00**

Facsimile
SHEPHERDS OF SUSSEX
Barclay Wills
Written as the last shepherds were disappearing from the rural scene, with notes on Michael Bland, John Dudeney, etc. Foreword by the Duke of Norfolk. The hill shepherd; lure of the shepherd's work; a character study of Sussex shepherds; shepherds of bygone days; the shepherd's possessions; crooks & bells; shearing; sheep washing, marking watering; dew-ponds; Sussex sheep; the crow-scarer, etc.
185 x 125mm   280 pages 28 B&W photos
Hardback ISBN 1 898941 60 2 Price **£20.00**
Paperback ISBN 1 898941 67 X Price **£8.95**

Facsimile
BLACK'S 1861 GUIDE TO SUSSEX
Incorporating 1859 Breads's guide to Worthing
and a description of the Miller's Tomb on Highdown Hill
This forms part of the South-Eastern Counties of England series and comprises 184 pages. There is a folding map of the county and steel engravings of the chain pier at Brighton, Hastings and Chichester cathedral. Major towns are covered as well as the smaller villages.

Paperback 210 x 148mm   276 pages Engravings and folding map
ISBN 1 898941 21 1   Price £8.95

Facsimile
THE HISTORY AND ANTIQUITIES OF HORSHAM
by Howard Dudley

This is a facsimile of one of the rarest and most sought-after topographical books on Sussex, first published in 1836 by a sixteen-year-old schoolboy. Illustrated with lithographs and wood engravings, the book covers the market town of Horsham and the surrounding villages of Rusper, Warnham, Roffy, Nuthurst, Itchingfield, Slinfold and Rudgewick.

Paperback 190 x 125mm   112 pages
ISBN 1 898941 72 6   Price £9.50

FROM SUSSEX YEOMEN TO GREENWICH WATERMEN
A W Gearing

Sussex 1500-1795. Greenwich 1795-1821. Greenwich 1821-1844. Greenwich 1844-1884. Greenwich 1884-1914. The Great War 1914-1922. Childhood memories 1922-1939. The war years 1939-1947. 1947-1985. Folkestone 1985 1997. Family tree.

Paperback 210 x 148mm   176 pages. Over 100 B&W photos
ISBN 1 898941 55 6 Price £10.00

A FULL LIFE IN DITCHLING, HASSOCKS AND BURGESS HILL 1919-1997
John Stenning

Ditchling, Sussex, between the wars. The farms, people 8 shopkeepers. Surrounding villages & towns.

Paperback 210 x 148mm   128 pages over 100 B&W photos
ISBN 1 898941 10 6   Price £5.95

A COUNTRYMAN'S FURTHER REMINISCENCES OF MID-SUSSEX
John Stenning

The South Downs • Farms 8 Farm folk • Early Days • Law abiding men • Ditchling Folk • Dumbrell's School Ditchling's Small Shops & Businesses • The Station Buses • Keymer & Hassocks Sussanah Stacey of Stanton's Farm Pouchlands Hospital Streat & Westmeston • Ditchling Pageant A Soldier's Diary

Paperback 210 x 148mm
160 pages over 100 B&W and 16 colour photos
ISBN 1 898941 42 4   Price £7.50

THE LIFE OF A MAN: RON SPICER 1929-1996
Dick Richardson & Doris Spicer

Ron Spicer was a herdsman at West Hoathly and a much loved folk singer. This memoir includes reminiscences from those who knew him, songs from the repertoire and pictures from the family album. Foreword by Baroness Trumpington.

Paperback 200 x 210mm   64 pages B&W photos
ISBN 1 898941 06 8   Price £6.50

All proceeds from the above title are donated to St Catherine's Hopsice, Crawley, who cared for Ron during his final days.

A DICTIONARY OF THE SUSSEX DIALECT
Rev WD PARISH
Edited by Dick Richardson

The dictionary was first published in 1875 by the vicar of Selmeston, the Rev WD Parish, following the pioneering work by Durrant Cooper. He also recorded provincialisms in use in the county at that time. This new edition is augmented by further pieces on the Sussex dialect, traditional recipes, and a mumming play from West Wittering from the writings of EV Lucas, who died in 1938. Illustrated throughout with line drawings of Sussex views made in the late 19th and early 20th centuries by Frederick L Griggs, ARA.

Paperback 220 x 150mm   192 pages 70 line drawings
ISBN 1 898941 68 8   Price **£7.50**

SUSSEX FOLK
THE FOLK SONG REVIVAL IN SUSSEX
Clive Bennett
Introduction by Shirley Collins

This book outlines the development of the folk song movement across Sussex from Chichester to Hastings with a detailed survey of the clubs in the densely populated central coastal area around Brighton. This ranges from the first Brighton skiffle club through the various other sessions in Brighton, Worthing, Eastbourne and Lewes up until the start of the new millennium. Within these pages are over 200 illustrations together with details of virtually all the clubs, venues, organisers and resident singers featured in the area for the past forty years.

Paperback 220 x 150mm   200 pages
ISBN 1 898941 78 5   Price **£14.95**

WRITING A BOOK?

Country Books is a small, independent publisher and has over 40 years publishing experience. In addition to our publishing activities, we undertake to produce books for other small publishers, individuals and societies (including the National Trust, Chatsworth House and Derbyshire County Council). This service began some years ago when we were submitted manuscripts which we felt worthy of publication but which, for one reason or another (usually because the likely print-run was too small to make it commercially viable), we were reluctant to take on under our own imprint. We would be pleased to assist you with the publication of your book. Please contact us for further information:

COUNTRY BOOKS
Courtyard Cottage, Little Longstone, Bakewell, Derbyshire DE45 1NN
Tel/Fax: 01629 640670 e-mail: dickrichardson@country-books.co.uk